Discourses
Volume One
2013–2014

DISCOURSES:
Living a Spiritually Rich Life
Volume One: 2013–2014

Yogacharya David R. Hickenbottom

Editor: Ruth M. Lamb, Ph.D

The Cross and The Lotus Publishing
Camano Island, Washington, USA

For permission requests, contact the publisher at:
http://www.crossandlotus.com/contact.html

ISBN: 978-1-957811-90-1 (softcover)
ISBN: 978-1-957811-91-8 (eBook)

All photos courtesy of Carla Hickenbottom Portfolio
unless otherwise attributed (see page 303)

Edited by Ruth Lamb

Book design by Jan Westendorp/Kato Design and Photo (katodesignandphoto.ca)

Cover design by Rob Landers, Ruth Lamb, and Jan Westendorp

Printed and bound in the USA

Published by
The Cross and The Lotus Publishing
Camano Island, Washington, USA
Website: www.crossandlotus.com

Contents

OM TAT SAT AUM

Preface

Yogacharya David, 2013.

These writings often come in the early morning: a time when the day is quiet and fresh, an open page upon which to write. These thought-expressions come from an unfathomable Source, welling up from the quiet of the all-pervading Spirit. Reading these words has the power to lead you to the same Source from which they have flowed from within me.

The inspiration that fuels these writings comes to me with great power and clarity, however mere words are incapable of holding all that is given. It is through inner attunement that the power in the words will lift you into the same Spirit that I experience in Super-consciousness—an uplifting power that is a passageway into realms divine.

Human words and thoughts are imperfect; it is only in pure Spirit that perfection is to be truly found. It is the purpose of these writings that we should rise together in the universal Spirit of God. Come, let us soar together and find truth and beauty unencumbered.

—YOGACHARYA DAVID

I n 2013, Reverend Yogacharya David Hickenbottom began post-ing brief discourses online on his blog, wherein he shared a portion of what God revealed to him through profound inner experience, as well as timeless practical wisdom for highest spiri-tual living in our day-to-day modern world.

Yogacharya David and his beloved wife, Carla, left on a pilgrim-age to India in September of 2013, and the discourses began as a medium by which friends and devotees could read about their travels and see photos taken along the way. The discourses con-tinued until 2019.

Very often, at God's prompting, Yogacharya David would write his discourses in the early hours of the day. Some would be com-pleted and sent not long after the sun had risen; more often, divine insights would develop over a period of days before taking final form. The spectrum of subjects he touched on was as broad as life itself—as infinite as God Himself. Whether a description of pure spiritual awareness, a moving tribute to his own guru, Mother Hamilton, the latest stop on their pilgrimage tour around North America, reflections on a book or movie, advice on mar-riage, the loss of friends and family, or updates on health, woven throughout every discourse was a constant theme of Love, Truth and Realized God-experience. The wisdom David gave voice to in his discourses harmonizes beautifully with the affirmation often stated by Mother Hamilton: God is life and life is God!

There were also special times when Yogacharya David would base his writing on a communication from a devotee, featuring what that one had given him which greatly touched his heart. The discourses were always accompanied by a beautiful picture carefully selected from his own photo catalogue or one found online that captured his inspiration.

Yogacharya David often gave a sermon on Sunday mornings, either in person to devotees or broadcast via YouTube. Many times, during the years after he began writing his discourses, Yogacharya David would read from his latest posting at the beginning of the talk. On occasion, God would then prompt him to weave the thread of the written discourse into broader subjects, with new and deeper dimension, as he spoke extemporaneously in these memorable Sunday Services.

For those who followed the discourses through the years as Yogacharya David posted them, and for readers who can now explore them in this series of publications, each missive takes us on the sacred climb from the human to the divine, discovering new reverence for this great pilgrimage we all share—our own life-journey. Yogacharya David's discourses lift the reader into an expansive view of God's fun and joy, unfolding surprising and delightful adventures around every corner. Equally, Yogacharya David speaks to the heart of the serious challenges and dark descents with which we all are faced from time to time, offering depths of insight into how to navigate the rough terrain and progress with steady steps toward the ultimate goal—the summit of God-realization.

This is the start of our six-volume discourse journey with Yogacharya David. With each volume he walks us up the sacred mountain of self-realization—he is at our side each step of the way. When he shares "alert here," he wants us to watch for, and to embrace, the lessons he embeds. Some are overt, many hidden, left for us to unravel ourselves as we embrace our Dharma and our own unique climb!

The titles for Yogacharya David's discourses seem to jump as living words from his writings. Enjoy, receive, and place his teachings within the context of your own unique life's plan. The six-volume series is outlined here:

- *Discourses—Volume One: 2013–14: Living a Spiritually Rich Life*

- *Discourses—Volume Two: 2015: Re-Union of Soul and Spirit*

- *Discourses—Volume Three: 2016: A True New Birth*

- *Discourses—Volume Four: 2017: Gateway to the Infinite*

- *Discourses—Volume Five: 2018: Standing on the Threshold of Eternity*

- *Discourses—Volume Six: 2019: Writing in the Book of Life*

The discourses are a precious fraction of Yogacharya David's legacy of teachings. Yogacharya David's writings come in many forms, such as hand written journals, handwritten teachings spanning many years, poetry, and writings stored on a number of computers, plus there approximately 1000 tape recordings of teachings he gave over the years both in Canada and in the United States. Additionally, as seva to the spirit within, never charging, Yogacharya David presented numerous workshops that offered pragmatic spiritual strategies for self-development and self-awareness.

In addition to this six-volume series of Discourses, Yogacharya David's poems are featured in *Climbing the Sacred Mountain: Poems and Prayers of a Western Yogi*; his journals and teachings from his 2000–2001 year of silence are featured in *Silence: Entering the Cosmic Sea of Consciousness*; moreover, the unique dharma teachings from that time are also, at his request, separately presented in *Notes to Sadhakas: How Dharma Works in Everyday Life*. *My Spiritual India* relates Yogacharya David's 1998–1999 inward and outward experiences during his spiritual journey to India. And as a daily feature to remind the soul of its active and welcome engagement in day-to-day life, an Infinite Calendar, titled *Touching the Supreme Spirit* provides daily inspiration. Over time, more of Yogacharya David's journals, teachings, and talks will be placed in texts for all to enjoy.

Yogacharya David's words are important, the essence, the meaning, and the power, so we have changed very few words in his writings. Spelling is corrected and grammar has been adjusted as required. We apologize for any errors, omissions, and request Guru's and reader's forgiveness.

It is a privilege to bring Yogacharya David's teachings forward to unify people of all faiths, people who seek a deeper relationship with the sacred, with the wisdom of our multidimensional self, and with the brilliant intelligence of Nature when She is honored as an important co-creative aspect of the Cosmic whole.

Regarding the use of images in this publication: Yogacharya David put great care, creativity, time, and intention into selecting images to complement his writings in each and every posting. When preparing his Discourses for publication, we found that certain images from unknown sources, or those which were found to be under copyright, could not be included. Every effort has been made to feature replacement images as close as possible to his original selections. In a few instances where no similar substitute was available, a picture of Yogacharya David or a beloved saint has been offered instead.[1] Substitute images are designated in the caption by a double asterisk **. For example: Image: Yogacharya David at Anandashram, 2005.** Image Attribution is available in the Reference section.

OM TAT SAT AUM

---

[1]   For more information about Yogacharya David and his writings, please visit www. crossandlotus.com

Introduction

Yogacharya David, Haridwar, India, 2005.

Dear Aspirant,

Whenever you begin a journey, you usually start with a destination in mind, a means of conveyance, and a map or landmarks to indicate that you are on the right path. Those of us following this path have God (Self) Realization as our Goal of goals. Our means of conveyance is God-remembrance, such as chanting God's Name, deepened meditation through Kriya Yoga, universal love and service, loving God, and discernment of Truth.

These discourses will act as markers upon your spiritual journey to make for safe and rapid progress. Unlike a scattered "hunt and peck" approach chosen by many, taking them on "wild goose chases" only to become thoroughly lost, you will receive teachings of the purest quality that speed you on the most direct path to realization. Obstacles arise which create challenges for your journey—you can find inspiration here to help you meet those challenges.

These writings contain notes from pilgrimages and journeys which also (reader alert here!) have lessons upon the path embedded in them.

With deepest love and blessings on your journey,
YOGACHARYA DAVID

LIVING A SPIRITUALLY RICH LIFE: 2013

September 6

My Gurudev: Truth Runs Clear

Mother Hamilton, 1977.

Truth runs clear, like pristine waters that sparkle in the sunlight. I drank deeply of those healing waters of Truth when I met my Gurudev. From my first meeting with her, I was exposed to words and concepts that came as new to me. As I proceeded with Mother, I understood more and more the depth of the ideas and profound divine wisdom she revealed to my thirsty soul.

From the beginning there was far more to Mother's communication than the amazing Truth of her words, for which she had gone through the jaws of death to realize. The Truth was profound enough, but the power of God was transferred as well to all who listened to her.

Through this power, I was lifted into higher states of consciousness. This sacred upliftment is what stood out to me time after time whenever I came into contact with my blessed Teacher. Power alone without clarity and purity of thought will go horribly awry. Mother had it all: power, wisdom, and purity, all aimed at the supreme goal of God-realization.

It is so rare on this earth to find this powerful, uplifting combination. Rarer yet is it to find this gift given in such a generous outpouring. It was a particular kindness to discover this divine incarnation of Truth in the form of a Western woman, not halfway around the world, but living and teaching nearby.

Gratitude wells up in an ocean of feeling, I pronam at her holy feet. Jai Guru! Victory to the Truth. My Gurudev has brought down truth from the highest heavens to this ailing earth for its total and complete recovery; that all may know of their sacred destiny.

September 13

THE POWER OF DIVINE LIFE

Divine blossoms.

There is a power, a pulsation that runs throughout all creation. When you awaken to the Divine Life your awareness of this power grows, sometimes within as it courses through your body and your being, and sometimes outside of your body through other people, in nature, even in human-made creations.

It is possible to be aware of this life-power without knowing its sacred roots, and this can be exhilarating, heady, or it can be terrifying and overwhelming. Either of these "ego" perceptions distorts the true nature of this power.

To know its true nature requires a stillness within, a listening heart and mind that is not consumed with the senses and worldly preoccupations. When you touch these realms, you are being exposed to the raw data that has formed this universe, not some-one's interpretation of how they say it is.

Your mental suppositions drop away, and you are now like a child being taken on a tour—you listen and learn. This aspect never changes; you are forever on the verge of understanding more, in constant awe of what is. Your entire being is lit up with a thrill and an expanding light that makes you feel there is no other place you would rather be than right where you are.

All pretense to be or know anything other than simply who you are right now is not allowed in this realm—this is your child-like nature. For those who choose such a life this experience is seen as a re-birth, as if you were just sleep walking before, and now you are awake! You have died to all the old pretenses and are born into your innate innocence.

Oh, there is nothing like it! And yet when you enter into this life you feel that this is the way it has always been, that any time of living outside of this awareness was just a temporary anomaly. The wounds and slashes of your past life that lived outside this Grace are not only healed but understood. You now walk in the power and grace of this Divine Life and you live in peace.

September 19

THE PILGRIMAGE TO INDIA BEGINS

Swami Satchidananda and Yogacharya David, 2007.

A pilgrimage begins long before you set foot out the door to go on one. It is best for a pilgrimage to originate as a calling, a deep inner prompting that goes beyond a yearning to travel and see new places. That is because a pilgrimage is a journey of the soul that takes on the guise of traveling to holy sites and meeting spiritual personalities.

A pilgrim is defined as one who travels to a shrine or holy place as a devotee[2] and the term pilgrimage is the journey of a pilgrim, which has been in use since the 1300s. Mother Hamilton

---

2   *Merriam-Webster Dictionary.*

recommended the book, *The Way of a Pilgrim*, which chronicles a Russian itinerate traveler who is inspired by St. Paul's admonition to pray without ceasing. In the Foreword by Father Thomas Hopko, he writes:

> . . . Life is communion with God: personal, direct, immediate, real, painful, peaceful, and joyful. It tells us that ceaseless prayer in pursuit of God and communion with Him is not simply life's meaning or goal, the one thing worth living for, but it is life itself. It tells us that Jesus Christ is this life, and that constant, continual, ceaseless prayer in His name opens the door to Divine reality and puts us in immediate contact with the One who is the source, substance, and goal of our life, and our very life itself.[3]

It is living in this "Divine reality" that guides and directs me in all my ways, and now it takes me back to the land Yoganandaji so beautifully described in the last words he uttered in his divine incarnation as he entered Mahasamadhi:

> The borderland of my India expanding into the world.
> Hail, mother of religions, lotus, scenic beauty, and sages!
> Thy wide doors are open,
> Welcoming God's true sons through all the ages,
> Where Ganges, woods, Himalayan caves and men
> dream God.
> I am hallowed; my body touched that sod![4]

---

3   *The Way of a Pilgrim* (Foreword).

4   *Whispers from Eternity* (p. 183).

When Swami Ramdas began his pilgrimage he was told inwardly that God, his Ram, was taking him all over India:

> If it was for sadhana, why should he go elsewhere? He could have practiced at home. Still God wanted him to go. Ramdas did not ask Him why he was being taken away, but He Himself whispered in Ramdas's ear: 'Ramdas, I am taking you from place to place not because you have to renounce everything, but because you have to see that everything is My form. You have to go to householders and tell them that they need not renounce worldly life in order to realize Me.'[5]

To begin with the right attitude and maintain it throughout the pilgrimage yields the greatest, the highest results; even as Papa so lovingly and dedicatedly followed to the letter his Ram's every command.

This is the fifth time that I have been directed to India: a spiritual homeland for me. Besides the tremendous ideals of Yoga, such as articulated in the Bhagavad Gita that have so deeply inspired me, there are also the holy sites and saints with whose darshan I have been blessed.

When I left Anandashram last, Swami Satchidananda, my second spiritual mother, said it was unlikely that we would meet again in the body. True to his word, he left the body since that last meeting. It was heart wrenching to leave him at that time, but I felt the inner direction to return to all of you, and I left with his kind permission.

Now, nearly seven years later, I am directed to return to India. Carla and I will spend some time up north for Lahiri Mahasaya's Mahasamadhi and birthday anniversaries, September 26th and

---

5   *Swami Ramdas on Himself* (p. 13).

30th, at Swami Keshabananda's ashram in Haridwar. We previously made friends with wonderful devotees there many years ago, and now we shall return. We will be staying at accommodations connected with Anandamayi Ma's Mahasamadhi Temple not far away in Kankhal. After a northern tour we will have the darshan of Swami Vishwananda in Bangalore and then arrive at the abode of bliss, Anandashram, in time for Swami Satchidananda's birthday celebration. There we plan to remain for the balance of our time in India, unless Ram directs otherwise, for we are forever at His whim.

As Papa said so truly, you do not need to leave hearth and home to practice God-remembrance. To make your life a sacred journey, regard each and every aspect of it as steps to your full realization, the attainment of your life's greatest aim.

I will take you in my heart, as I know I shall remain in yours. In the constant thought of the One may you be forever blessed in your pilgrimage back to your complete God-realization.

September 25

WITH GOD AS OUR TOUR GUIDE!

Elephant statue at Akshardham Temple.

With God as our tour guide there is no end to the delight He takes in surprising and delighting us on our journey. We had some practical tasks we had to take care of on our first day in India, and then we thought we would take a car and driver for half the day while we are in Delhi.

Operating on about three hours of sleep but desirous to reset our body clocks to the twelve-and-a-half-hour time difference, we asked at the hotel about going to see the large Hanuman figure and temple here in Delhi. A dozen years ago we had the darshan of this monkey-king and foremost devotee of Ram in the form of this gigantic statue: he is covered in red and stands about 40 feet tall: an impressive divine image. However, no one here knew of this temple. The travel guide had a different idea, pointing to a map that indicated a newer temple complex about 15 kilometers away. I somehow felt an attraction to going.

We hired the car and driver for about 5 dollars an hour and set off on a Ram adventure. The large temple complex loomed ahead as we drove on an elevated freeway. This is one of the many differences that has occurred in the last 15 years that I have been coming to India. The elevated freeway is a stark contrast to the potholed roads where wandering cows were a regular feature.

The name of the mandir complex is Swaminarayan Akshardham. Now, many of you will be familiar with Swami Narayan through the DVD entitled *Mystic India*. Unbeknownst to us when looking at the map along with the travel guide, we were being directed to the mandir of the very same saint.

The temple complex is breathtaking, and its creation is equally remarkable. In five years, from November 2000 to November 2005, Swami Maharaj (Swamishri) led the effort to transform 100 acres of desolation into a manicured park with the largest Mandir in India, complete with 300,000 carved stones within the complex. The workmanship is exquisite.

The architecture and artisanship are outstanding. This work is not merely an empty shell of piled stones, as has been the case with other temples I have had the opportunity to see. Inside the mandir stand the carved images of Rama, Sita, and Hanuman, the likenesses of Krishna and Radha, Parvati, and Mahadev Shiva— all manifest a strong life-force that brings devotion to the heart and soul.

How can 300-million work hours be so purely dedicated to a higher ideal? It must mean that it was truly a labor of love. This stands as a challenge to each of us to do better, to strive for more, and to manifest divine beauty in all that we do. It was remarkable that this vast temple complex was done in 5 years; as Satish Gujaral, an internationally known architect, opined, "It could have taken 50 years to build such a thing."

It seems that God has taken an interest in connecting us with saint Swami Narayan to whom this Temple is dedicated and who was the subject of the *Mystic India* film that I had watched with interest a few times. At the center of the large and extensively beautiful mandir is a statue of the saint, eleven feet tall and glowing in gold.

If you have seen *Mystic India* you may remember the shots taken at a temple with ornate figures carved in the pillars. I can tell you many of these scenes were definitely filmed on location here and that even though the Imax film is most beautifully crafted, still it does not do full justice to the exquisite art.

There is a ride on a boat that is part of the Temple complex that is reminiscent of Disneyland's Pirates of the Caribbean, in that you float in a boat through a tunnel complex filled with 800 life-like statues that depict 10,000 years of India's history and her contributions to the world. We first saw an ancient Vedic village, then the world's first university that was in existence for 1300 years. India's contributions to astronomy, mathematics, including the invention of the number zero, and the world's first hospital. The many interesting advancements include India's most important contribution, the philosophy and practical techniques of Yoga for advancing human evolution, dating back at least five thousand years.

But what stands out to both Carla and I from our time at Swami Narayan's Temple complex is the feeling of purity we felt when moving through the sacred sites of the mandir. Surely some great souls have been involved in its creation. We pronamed in reverence to these divine images of Rama, Krishna, and Shiva, and their divine consorts, and we felt blessed for being taken to a place of honor for Swami Narayan.

One additional travel note: As we were completing our "in-air travel" of twenty hours while flying over Varanasi, we were witness to an extraordinary occurrence. Looking south out of the window I glimpsed some flashes of light. Thinking at first that it was the plane's flashing light reflecting off the clouds, I then looked closer; the clouds were too far away to be reflecting the plane's lights. The intensity of the bright flashes grew, along with the rapidity of the flashing. The clouds that lit up were at a great distance, and even though they looked about even with us, I think they must have been lower in altitude as we were at about 35,000 feet at the time. It became clear that these were cloud-to-cloud lightning strikes at some distance and stretched as far left and right as we could see.

If you could imagine a dangling jellyfish thousands of feet high that suddenly was so brilliantly illuminated within that all that remained, other than an incredibly bright light, were the gray and black outlines of the edges of the jellyfish, or in this case, thunder heads, then you can imagine the terrifying beauty of this display.

The flashes were too fast to count and lit up vast regions of space. From left to right, in the center, and then spasmodically back to the right, and so on, the lightning was working at a furious pace that left us speechless with wonder; and yet the plane was totally unaffected by this violent storm. It was one of the most awe-inspiring sights of nature to which I have been a witness. Carla and I were the only ones with our window shade open and may have been the only ones, except for the pilots, to see this incredible display of Mother Nature! This was our welcome back to India, the place of wonders and glories from time immemorial, and it still is!

September 29

HARIDWAR

Lahiri Mahasaya: Painting in Mandir.

Before dawn, we were off to the New Delhi train station for our journey to Haridwar. Haridwar is an ancient pilgrimage site for Hindus where the Ganges tumbles out of the Himalayas and flows out onto the flat plains and eventually disgorges into the enormous Bay of Bengal.

Over a hundred years ago Swami Keshabananda, exalted disciple of Lahiri Mahasaya, established an ashram there. Our pilgrimage to Haridwar coincides with the Mahasamadhi anniversary of Lahiri Mahasaya.

God is ever testing his devotees to "be in the world, but not of it." The porter who grabbed our bags and took them to the train wanted 650 rupees, an exorbitant sum for such a service. I asked around and found a reliable source who said 50 rupees was about standard, although it could vary.

Entering the train car, he deposited our largest case above the seat and demanded his ransom. Offering him the 50 rupee note, he argued and feigned walking out of the car, trying to make us believe he was so insulted by this amount it was not worth taking. "The game was afoot!" I always want to pay what is reasonable, but not respond to extortionate greed.

Once I was negotiating with an auto-rickshaw driver, he demanded twenty thousand rupees to take me to my destination. Having asked fellow riders before departing from the train I knew that the amount should be about 20 rupees. I told him that I was not asking to buy his auto-rickshaw, only to get a ride in it! He laughed and I offered 20 rupees, and with a wobble of his head he answered me, "Ok."

Delhi is different; these porters are known to be aggressive. After he feigned walking away, he returned; I offered 70 rupees, he lowered his demand from 650 to 200; I handed him 100, which he took, and he walked away in a huff. With Westerners, many people in service here have learned that whatever they ask will be paid; after all, as a foreigner how would you know any different? However, when you are called on your bluff, why continue to make it a difficult situation? There is no joy in the interaction. Immediately after, an Indian family boarded with four porters, and a similar verbal tussle ensued. After paying 500 rupees for the four porters, they left in a similar state of apparent unhappiness.

Life is not meant to be lived in such a way. There is nothing wrong with negotiating for a wage and asking for what you want; however, when there is no expressed joy in the interchange, then the participants are left feeling worse off for the service. All service, whether it is for seva only or in exchange for money, should be saturated with love and joy. In this way both the giver and the receiver are enriched by the experience.

There are many sorts of poverty, but to be devoid of joy and love in the service to humans is one of the worst forms of poverty known to humankind; it is a poverty of the soul. It is a challenge to the devotees to hold their ground for what is reasonable, and not get caught up in the drama of emotional blackmail that is designed to make them feel uncomfortable and therefore yield to the coercion; a challenge to remain joyful in all circumstances.

Finally, we are on our way in the train. There is something quite wonderful about the rocking and rolling of a train and the clickity-clack of the rails below. The scenery changes from rough-and-tumble buildings and strewn trash that lines the railways in town to neatly tended farms dotting the countryside. Four hours of progress, the last hour going backwards, takes us to our destination.

Upon arriving at the Haridwar station the normal din of activity is all about, and we are approached by those who would provide taxi or auto-rickshaw rides, but our first order of business is to buy return tickets. As we stand at the window to make reservations, suddenly all three clerks behind the heavily barred windows disappear. It seems it is lunch time and while the other patrons will wait patiently for the one-hour break, we decide to move on to Anandamayi Ma's ashram where we have reservations to stay.

A pleasant-looking gentleman is standing near us, and I ask him what I should pay for an auto-rickshaw ride to Ma's ashram. He asks a few questions and tries to call the phone numbers we have been given for the ashram, but no answer; he thinks some numbers are missing. He so lovingly takes us in hand, guides us out to an extended version of an auto-rickshaw, bargains with the driver for us, writes down the rickshaw number and name, and tells us to pay the driver 100 rupees when we arrive.

My heart is overwhelmed with this "stranger's" sense of hospitality for us, for his selfless service to "God's little children" who have come without arrangements. I tell him a heartfelt, "God bless you," and he smiles so sweetly and pronams to us. We feel so blessed by the masters who have come in the form of this wonderful soul; may he truly be blessed for his wonderful kindness of heart.

In Delhi we had been in taxis, but now in the auto-rickshaw we feel more part of the fabric of the town. The smells, sights, and people are so tangible. One of the unique aspects of India is the smell. At its best it is a combination of the spices, the sweet smell of burning dung in the air and a combination of a thousand-thousand smells—that is the signature of being in India.

The auto-rickshaw is a three-wheeled contraption that runs on a tiny two-stroke engine; the single front wheel can make the vehicle turn within its own diameter, which makes it very flexible. The spatial sense of drivers in India is remarkable; there is one scene after another of auto-rickshaws, pedestrians, cars, cows, pigs, dogs, and lorries all competing for space and movement and all within inches of one another, with bumpers that read, "please honk!" For honking is not an angry form of communication here; rather, it is saying, "I am passing you, be aware," or "I am beside you, don't move further over!" And so on. It all adds to the sense of complete pandemonium of traffic here as the auto-rickshaw takes us on main roads and alleys through a confusing maze.

Even though it seems there are no rules to driving here, really there are definite rules of the road, only just very different from Western sensibilities. It is true for both personal space as well as vehicular space; if there is an inch of empty space between you and the next person or vehicle, then that is considered wasted space, and therefore space to be utilized.

I remember my father reprimanding me as a child while standing in line, saying, "Give some space to those people in front of you." This was considered being polite. If I had been raised in India, my father would have given me a wave of the hand indicating get in closer, you are wasting space and besides, someone will just move in front of you if you leave extra space. It is a diametrically opposite value and takes some getting used to.

We arrive at Ma's Temple site and we immediately feel the difference. The hotel in Delhi was nice but filled with a business class of Indians and the energy that brings. When we enter the rooms here, there is a spiritual vibrancy immediately noticeable, like arriving home. Anandamayi Ma's pictures are everywhere, her beauty inside and out is evident in the images of her great incarnation.

After being settled, we are anxious to go to Keshavashram. We once again enter the precincts of this holy ground, after an eight-year absence. Both Babaji and Lahiri Mahasaya have blessed this ground. A profusion of garlands and scattered petals are signs that this is special day, the Mahasamadhi anniversary of Lahiri Baba. Like a magnet we are drawn directly to his Samadhi temple on the grounds: a small structure about 12 feet tall that contains some of the ashes of the great master.

At the time of Lahiri Mahasaya's passing, he had requested of his wife that he be buried; not cremated. In India children under seven and swamis are buried, all others are cremated. In her grief, she did not remember his request; only after his cremation did she remember. Swami Keshavananda knew his master was getting ready to shed his mortal coil and was getting ready to embark on the long journey to Benares. Lahiri Mahasaya physically manifested before Swami Keshavananda to tell him not to hurry, he had already departed his physical frame. Our guide at the ashram tells us that the very ashoka tree standing here is where Lahiri Mahasaya appeared to Swami Keshavananda. The Swami did go on to Benares and returned with some of the ashes of his master's cremated body. He then built this small temple in honor of his spiritual master.

Meditating in front of the master's Samadhi Temple, we felt his Presence glowing and shining upon us. Flocks of parrots flew by, and a smaller bird seemed to take an interest in us. He landed on a nearby wire, then hopped to the ground and chirped and frolicked in front of us. As sometimes happens, it seemed that the bird's activities were not unconnected with our being there in honor of the master. Animals oftentimes respond to devotion in uncanny ways, and great masters will even occasionally manifest as an animal, or any form, in order to enact a play with devotees. We felt bathed in the spiritual vibrancy of these hallowed grounds.

We toured the grounds and observed that they have made improvements in the garden, which is looking very nice. However, back by the sacred rudraksha and banyan trees that in the past had been a scene of worship, now this area was being used as a garbage dump; how strange, and how instructive. That, what at one time was sacred ground can become a dumping ground for the garbage of life. This can happen to a piece of property, and it can happen to a person when sadhana is not maintained at its proper intensity.

When we checked in at Ma's ashram, Dr. Ghosh of the International Center, recommended that we see a lady saint, Rani Ma, who lived at Keshavashram for ten years without leaving the grounds. She now has an ashram of her own and he said he would contact a driver who knew how to get there. That driver was not available, so there was a long conversation between Keshab, the lovely man who runs the day-to-day workings of this devotee hotel, and the taxi driver. A long conversation usually does not bode well for arriving at the right place in India, but we set off in anticipation of meeting the saint.

From Keshavashram, we drive for some distance toward Rishikesh and finally we enter into some very narrow streets. Parked cars leave just enough space for our Toyota SUV to pass with our mirrors pulled in. The ability of the Indian driver to "thread the needle" of these streets is breathtaking.

At times, the driver looks to us to see if we are going to the right place, and with some concern we assure him we have absolutely no idea of where we are at, much less where we should go! With some stopping to ask for directions, we at last come to the gates of Rani Ma's ashram. We are led through quaint gardens where we remove our chappals (shoes). We are led through narrow sidewalks and finally to a small courtyard where the saint is seated. She is surrounded by a couple dozen devotees, women on one side and men the other. We take our seats.

A pleasant man sitting next to me takes an interest in us, we being the only Westerners in attendance. He offers to introduce us. For some reason the name Carla is difficult for many Indians to pronounce. I think it may be the placement of the r; Kali comes easily, but Carla is difficult. He proceeds to sit next to Rani Ma. From our arrival, I can see she has something, and a kind of spiritual power is coming out in waves. She speaks no English, and appears to be averse to looking straight at me, perhaps a natural sense of reserve.

We are invited to come forward and have her darshan. When I sit in front of her, her legs are stretched out but I am told not to touch her feet. She is dressed in a new sari. A tiny woman, she looks to be swimming in gold-trimmed cloth. She looks off to the side, never directly at me. She appears to be quite old, but clearly, she has a lively mind and presence.

I tell her we have come for her blessings. The interpreter translates, "I have no blessings to give; Bhagwan has already blessed you." After some time of sitting with the saint we take our leave, feeling blessed by her presence. Our kind interpreter guides us to an area to take some Prasad made by a joyful lady devotee there. Our guide tells us he has been seeing Rani Ma for over ten years. He says, "I have been getting older; we have all been getting older, but Rani Ma does not get any older. She is known to be over 100 years old, but no one knows for sure how old she is."

There are small red lights that decorate the path going back out of the garden area, taking us out into the black night. Here, in this simple ashram, God has taken us to the heart of India. The display of a natural love for saints, and the desire for their darshan and blessings, is in the heart-blood of spiritual India.

These devotees have an unaffected relationship with Rani Ma, speaking with ease, laughter, and naturalness that make the idea of walking and talking with Jesus, or Buddha, as natural as being with the best of friends. This world would be manifestly better if there were this kind of natural love and regard for saints exhibited everywhere. The blessings that flow from them are a boon of inestimable value for a world drowning in separation from self, Self, and from God. Surely, with this love for saints, their blessings flow even more abundantly to one and all. Rani Ma's words ring still: "Bhagwan (God) alone bestows the blessings, and all that is to be given has already been given."

September 29

BLESSINGS

Anandamayi Ma.

The service begins at 7 a.m., just when we arrived at Anandamayi Ma's Samadhi Temple near Haridwar in Kankhal. Sanskrit chanting fills the air, and a dozen boys sit in front of us accompanying the priest in the chants.

I was immediately taken inward and with stunning clarity, Ma spoke to me wordlessly, "It is the same Light that manifests in all realized masters, and all realized souls experience the same God."[6] This universalizing of truth takes away all sense of "I and mine" and leads to complete universal freedom.

---

6   As I said, this communication came wordlessly, so I am forced to give words to a wordless communication.

Then the thought of Christine came to mind; the picture Carla had brought of her appeared clearly to my inner vision. I knew that I did not need to ask for anything, only to just hold her in mind in this experience with Ma. Tremendous blessings were accomplished in that moment.

For the first hour I was completely engrossed in my experience with Ma. In the second hour a woman sang the most haunting, lovely tune as part of the aarti.[7] Every sound found resonance in my heart center and as each part of the heart was touched through her song, a particular light lit the corresponding region of my heart. One part of the heart glowed, gold, then another part was lit with deep red, another indigo, and so on. It was a most beautiful experience as my heart center itself was responding to the beautiful notes of the lady singer.

Of course, the ceremony was all in Sanskrit, which I do not know. However, the entire ritual is designed to bring you closer to Ma and her blessings. All religious ceremonies are designed, or should be, to bring you closer to God, and if it does not accomplish its goal then the ceremony has failed you. This same principle is also true for every experience in life; all experiences should bring you closer to God. So, do not be thrown by the endless variety life displays to you; each experience is a test for you to see the Divine Spirit in every aspect of His creation.

Our friend Ram Alexander played a central role in building the International Center where we are staying. Ma had indicated that she wanted high-quality sattvic facilities for foreigners to stay in while doing their spiritual practices near the temple here. The people in charge, Dr. Ghosh and his able assistant, Keshab (for whom I feel such great love), and the other workers here are

---

7   Aarti, meaning "complete love," is a ritual of waving lamp lights in front of an altar or deity.

blessed with the spirit of seva. With a bright smile and a pronam, nothing is too much to ask for.

We continue to have evolving plans for our time in India. However, we have been in India just three days, but already it feels like at least a month!

While attending the evening aarti, Ma has continued her joyful revelations to me. As I sit and the rituals proceed, different ones come and go; a tour group even walks through during the sacred ceremony, glancing at the temple like a tourist attraction. Some of these spiritual tourists quickly pronam in response to the ongoing chanting and move through, and others come and sit for a few minutes and then leave; children seem to having no understanding at all of why they are here or of what is occurring.

What Ma reveals during all of this activity is that all the forms, the priest, the boys chanting, the people coming and going, are all her forms. I clearly perceive the depth of this truth: that alternating between forms of ignorance and devotion, all are her manifestations.

The lesson that all are her forms continues with me past the aarti, right to the time when we return to the International Center for our meal. Ma comes in the form of a long-term traveler to India who sits with us for dinner. He tells us about his many years of coming to India, and that on several occasions he tried to see Ma in Delhi when she was still in the body, however it never worked out for them to meet.

He had a guru he had been deeply devoted to from Bengal, but he said, that was in the past, "enough said." Clearly something unsavory had occurred to put him off of him. Now he is attracted to the teachings of Ramana Maharshi. Perhaps that feels like a safe outlet for his desire for God.

His situation makes me appreciate what an incredible blessing it has been to have Mother in my life, as well as having the role

Swami Satchidananda played in my quest for realization. This traveler seems like a lost soul, missing his heart's true desire.

However, seeing him clearly as Ma coming in his form, my prayer goes out to the all-beneficent Creator that this man, this manifestation of Ma, should find what he surely is looking for. And, being a manifestation of Ma, I have no fear for him, no fear at all, for Ma will call her own back to her Self. My only thought, which is put into my mind by the universal compassion of the infinite, is that he attain the happiness, peace, bliss, and joy for which he so clearly yearns. Jai Ma!

October 1

A DEVOTEE AND MA

Center spire at the top of Anandamayi Ma's Mahasamadhi Temple.

Editor's Note: David recounts the following narrative told to him by a devotee of the International Centre, Anandamayi Ma Ashram, Kankhal, India.

Do you know how I became a disciple of Ma's? When I was a little boy, seven or eight years old maybe, we lived here in Haridwar, the first Bengali family living here. Now, my mother always told me to bow at the feet of my elders; if I didn't, I was in trouble with her.

Anandamayi Ma came here for two weeks after a disciple gave her some property, an old temple. Ma, being Bengali, came to my mother's notice, and my mother was told, "You should go and see her; she is a holy person." So, my mother took me to see her.

When I saw Ma, I saw her as only an old woman, but I knew I should touch her feet as my mother taught me to do to my elders. However, the people around Ma said that no one should touch her feet. I was worried that I would be in trouble with my mother for not paying my respects to Ma, so I went around behind her and reached down to touch her feet. I wasn't thinking of her being anyone special. I was only thinking that I did not want to get in trouble with my mother!

When Ma turned around to see who had touched her feet, she saw me and threw me a flower; but the other ladies with her were scolding me, saying I was a naughty boy. All I knew was that now I would not be in trouble with my mother. Now, I think it was on that day that I received diksha (initiation) from Ma.

I did not have any strong connection with Ma until I got married. The way I met my wife was that my brother was in the market one day and a gentleman from Nepal heard him speaking and said, "Oh, you are from Bengal!" Since both were Bengalese, they struck up a conversation. The man had a daughter he wanted to marry to a Bengali, but not to someone from the big city of Calcutta. The families met later, and everything was arranged for our marriage.

When we had been married for just three days, there was a celebration for Ma's birthday. (I believe in the doctor's narrative that Ma had left the body by this time.) My mother was making a mala (a circle of flowers) for Ma's anniversary, and my wife asked my mother if she would show her how to make one as well. My mother had a lot of ego at that time, and she told my wife that she did not have time right then, but after the celebrations she would take the time to teach her.

My wife felt very bad about this as her family had left to go back to Nepal and she was feeling very lonely. She went to our room and saw Ma's picture there. She did not feel any connection with Ma at the time, but she talked to the picture, "Ma, I respect you because you are the guru of my husband's family. I want to make a mala for you, but I do not know how. Will you teach me?"

My wife suddenly knew how to make the mala; she even made hers faster than my mother did! My wife was quite excited by this and wanted to present her mala before my mother presented hers. So, we got to the temple a little bit before my mother, and she gave her mala to Ma's Samadhi site. When my mother presented hers, she noticed there was already one on the altar and she wondered who could have done this work, as she thought she was the only one who could do it this way.

Afterward, my mother commented on the other mala and my wife told her it was hers. When she asked how it could be done, my wife told her the whole story. It was then that my wife told me that I should have a special regard for Ma, our family guru.

After my son graduated with a master's degree, he had a bad time. He was depressed. It was terrible. I was so worried for him. I went to Ma's picture and told her that she needed to help him without the need for doctors or hospitals. I demanded this from Ma as a son can demand from a mother; not asking but telling.

Ma told me, "He needs to change his house." I went to some astrologers, and they said the same thing. So, I flew to Bangalore where my son was. It cost me one lakh of rupees to do all of this, and we changed his house. When my son walked into the new house, he asked my wife, "Mommy, would you make me some tea?" She had tears streaming down as she made his tea; she was so happy. The next day, he asked for food, and after that, he was all right! Jai Ma.

At one time, I knew it was time to take initiation; Swami Baskarananda[8] was the right person to do it. I went to the temple early in the morning with my beads and was chanting so intensely to prepare myself for initiation. I was sitting in front of Ma's picture, and she actually came out of that picture and touched me on the shoulder. She said, "Not too much." I saw her come out; I felt her hand on my shoulder!

I then went to see Swami Baskarananda. When I stood outside his closed door, he called out my name. I did not usually go to temple; I was so surprised to hear him call my name. Then he opened his door, and he asked me in. I was so shocked! I wanted to tell him what had happened with Ma and that I had come for initiation. I started to speak and Swamiji held up his hand, saying, "I know, I know." I started to tell him anyway when he held up his hand again and said, "Ma was here. She told me everything."

Ma had given Swamiji everything before she left the body. He knew what I had come for and initiated me without being told anything. Jai Ma!

---

8   Swami Baskarananda was an advanced disciple of Ma's and highly respected by her followers. The Swami left his body not long ago.

October 1

MA'S LILA AND LAHIRI MAHASAYA'S BLESSINGS

Yogacharya David and Rakesh standing under the Ashok
Tree where Lahiri Mahasaya appeared, in his physical
body, to Swami Keshabananda after his Mahasamadhi.

Without knowing why God was directing our feet in pilgrimage to India, I have remained a simple and open child of the Infinite for His will to be done. I knew I wanted to be in Haridwar for Lahiri Mahasaya's Mahasamadhi Day. We experienced such blessings from the master and felt him in such a wonderful way at Keshavashram. In past pilgrimages, I have stayed near this ashram, but this time we were directed to Anandamayi Ma's Samadhi Temple some distance away in Kankhal.

Here we were to become a part of Ma's Lila, her divine play. Every morning and evening there is an elaborate aarti, a ceremony of worship. The Samadhi Temple is an extravagant display of marble, beautifully constructed. In the Sanctum Sanctorum there is a statue of Ma ensconced in a humble thatched hut: a fitting symbol of her humble birth and the way she lived her life.

There are different singers whose voices are broadcast on speakers, and a couple dozen boys, dressed in gold, who accompany the singer. A priest is in front and center and arranges all the articles of worship. Ma was a respecter of Brahmanic law and Vedic rituals, keeping their notions of propriety and purity. While she lived her life spontaneously, inspired by God alone, the rules of Temple culture are strictly governed by protocol.

Ideally, the Brahman priest is a keeper of the sacred vibrations of the temple. He will care for the deity and the area around it, following strict rules. These rules are designed to keep the vibrations pure and ensure that blessings will be transferred to devotees worshiping there. Lighted lamps and other articles of worship are offered to the deity and then given out in blessings to the attendees.

In these precincts, we feel Ma's presence so greatly. She is a living voice and presence in my mind, and she effortlessly guides me in inner experiences with a purity and purpose that comes absolutely from the highest planes of consciousness. For a great Soul such as Ma, physical death is of no import. Her consciousness, presence, and divine purpose are fulfilled to any heart and soul sensitively attuned to God.

On the last night of aarti, Ma once again is present. Her smiling presence greets me through her picture and soon I am lifted beyond all sensory and supersensory experience. I am merged into the eternal Being and Presence of the ultimate, all-conscious Existence. No words may encroach into this beginingless, endless Source of all that is. In this state of Consciousness, no rituals intrude, and no relationship of I and Thou can enter, only Oneness. I remain absorbed in this state throughout the aarti.

At another time, we tour Ma's museum: it holds many personal items and pictures of Anandamayi Ma. After touring the inside of the museum, we enter the grounds where we are engaged by an elderly man whose few teeth go in every-which direction. He has a wonderful glow about him. He speaks no English but kindly offers to be our guide to the museum grounds.

He leads us past a pond that has unusual leaves; we are told later that these are blue lotus plants, not yet in bloom. He then takes us to the Panchavati, a sacred grove of five trees, each specified species must be present to be considered a Panchavati. As we follow our guide, we are charmed by this old man and the grounds. We then come to a building that was deconstructed in Delhi and re-erected here; it is a quaint hut where Ma lived while in Delhi. It has a wonderful vibration to it.

A young man from the museum joins us and gives us some information in English. He tells us, "Do you know how old he is?" Referring to our guide. He answers his own question, "He is one hundred and ninety-seven."

I ask, "Ninety-seven?" He says, "No, one hundred and ninety-seven!" Well, in the country of India, one can come to believe in the miraculous around every corner.

Next to the hut are steps down to the Ganges. We descend to the riverside, and it is here that we enact a ritual for Christine, dipping her laminated picture into the Ganges in this spot blessed by Ma. As in past pilgrimages, we have felt the purifying nature of the Ganges. We ask Ganga Ma to so bless Christine that she may be cleansed of everything that is not of God. Om Sri Ram Jai Ram Jai Jai Ram. We then baptize our own heads and bodies in the sacred stream.

Walking up the steps, there is a temple of Ganga Ma. She is a beautiful image; symbolically, she represents the flow of life-force in the spine. By uplifting that life-current, the individual soul is baptized in the healing currents of Prana, the Divine Life within and without.

As I think about our time in Haridwar/Kankhal, it has come unexpectedly for us to enter into Ma's Lila here, but what a delightful, powerful, and gracious play she has enacted within and without. Jai, Ma! Victory to the Divine Mother!

"We take our leave of Kankhal, but not of you, Ma." We have also felt the ongoing Presence of our dear beloved Lahiri Baba. To stand under the ashok tree where he manifested to Swami Keshabananda and to be transported to his feet at his Samadhi Temple—these are blessings we hold close to our hearts as we board the train for Delhi and new adventures.

October 3

DAKSHINESWAR YOGODA SATSANG

Yogoda Satsanga Math at Dakshineswar.

Feeling Mother's guidance around travel arrangements and places to stay, we have upgraded our travel in India for this pilgrimage. In the past, it has been local buses, train travel, and generally low-priced hotels that we have stayed in. This pilgrimage has seen us take advantage of nice, but not top-of-the-line hotels, and we have flown from Delhi to Kolkata (the updated spelling of Calcutta). This has certainly smoothed out travel, decreased some of the stress, and made it generally easier on the physical body as well as the subtle energy body.

Our first full day here came on a holiday, the birth of Mahatma Gandhi. This great soul has become the world's archetype for ahimsa: the removal of violence from the heart and the integrity of living a God-centered life. He chanted Ram Nam, daily read from the Bhagavad Gita, and practiced deepened meditation. Surely, he was a great (Mahatma) soul.

Early in the a.m., we traveled to Yogoda Satsanga Society (Self-Realization Fellowship (SRF) of India) Ashram. Master saw this property on the Ganges in Dakshineswar for sale when he was here in 1935–6 and we are told he arranged for its purchase when he returned to the US.

We had made an inquiry about staying at this ashram by phone and we were told by the gruff swami on the phone that only SRF members may stay here. It always feels like a loss that there is this lack of connection made by this organization with those who have great love and devotion for Master. Long ago, SRF chose this path, and it is a loss for both sides of the issue.

I do not think this organization would have any difficulty with the idea that Swami Pranabananda, Swami Keshabananda, and Swami Sri Yukteswarji (all disciples of Lahiri Mahasaya) did not exist under a single umbrella of a common organization, or that any one of them would be wrong for continuing Lahiri Mahasaya's teachings. Yet, and perhaps this is so embedded in Western thinking that it seems to be a natural course of events, organizations mark out a territory and say, "You either belong to us or you are out." As Mother said, even though they put us out, Mother drew a circle and drew them in.

The beautiful mandir has a large, many-pillared porch area, and inside there are pictures of the masters in front. We sat in blissful contemplation for some time, feeling Master's blessings and those of our guru-lineage. Such a feeling of peace pervaded us as we sat, then as we walked in silence throughout the grounds.

An East-Indian devotee from Malaysia spoke with us; he was very sweet. And the young man in the bookstall was also a pleasure to speak with. Really, true devotees of God may be found anywhere, and there are many roads to realization. God knows the heart, and no one may gainsay or pre-judge anyone based on affiliation or non-affiliation with any group or religion. The sooner we look through "the eyes of God" and into the heart and soul of anyone we meet, the surer will be our discrimination.

How wonderful it is that Mother freed us of being in or out, for God is our focus, and therefore everyone is in—if there is an "in" to be found. To universalize our vision and see God everywhere is our aim. Lovers of God, by whatever name He may be called, can be recognized in any soul, whatever the language, manner of dress, or name.

Surely one of God's greatest attributes is peace, shanti, the peace that surpasses all understanding. It was Master's blessing to saturate us with that peace and for us to feel it in every step we took on those ashram grounds. Having spent an uplifting time there, we moved on to the Kali Temple, carrying that peace with us through the bumpy, noisy, crowded streets of Dakshineswar.

October 3

THE KALI TEMPLE OF DAKSHINESWAR

Sri Ramakrishna Paramhansa, 1879.

We come to a street that is crowded on both sides with stalls carrying all manner of religious pictures and instruments. Red and white, gold and orange colors are festive reminders, displayed in the stalls that are filled with devotional paraphernalia. We crept through the gates and parked, then walked some distance in the tropical sun on our way to the Kali Temple.

This Kali Temple complex was to be the home and witness of the great spiritual master Ramakrishna Paramhansa. The teachings of this God-man can be read in *The Gospel of Sri Ramakrishna* by Master Mahasaya, of whom Master so lovingly wrote about in Chapter 9 of the *Autobiography of a Yogi* as "The Blissful Devotee and His Cosmic Romance."[9] I have read *The Gospel* many times and I can pick it up and start reading anywhere; it truly is a Gospel. Master also had the vision of the Divine Mother here when he came with his sister in response to her plea to help reform her husband.

Entering the Temple grounds is a reminder of the times we live in as metal detectors, dogs, and guards seek out detection of any *non-devotional* materials upon your person. Entering into the compound, we come to the main Kali Temple. The devotion of the Hindu is really wonderful to see. Armed with flowers and contributions of money, the devotees wait patiently in the sun for a glimpse of the terrifying deity.

Kali is perhaps one of the most difficult icon-mysteries to penetrate. Bloody extended tongue, wearing skulls, and wielding a sword, she is fierce. Decapitating the head and wearing it is symbolic of the death of the ego, but one must steadfastly be willing to enter her *killing grounds* to go beyond the awful exterior and discover the beautiful universal Divine Mother who resides within the fearsome exterior.

We view the deity that Ramakrishna worshiped. She is indeed a wonderful image of God in an extensive sea of icons of Hindu images. We move on to another temple within the complex. Here is the black-faced Krishna and Radha whom Ramakrishna originally served as a priest. Both Carla and I felt tremendous power, Shakti, emanating from this beautiful image of Krishna standing with flute in hand and lustrous eyes.

Who can explain how an image of stone, metal, and cloth can become a Source of divine Shakti? However, what I can say is that

---

9   *Autobiography of a Yogi* (p. 75).

I have experienced the reality of this power on several occasions, where an image, a picture, or a place will evoke a powerful spiritual experience. A person, place, or image can indeed become a source of blessing for those who are attuned to its vibrations. For us, this Krishna and Radha radiate this power and we were blessed by its Grace. We toured the multiple temples with Shiva Lingas and went down to the Ganges for some water on the feet and on top of the head.

Then we enter the room where Ramakrishna lived for so many years in the corner of the Temple complex. I have been here once before, fifteen years previous. I remember at the time, yearning to spend more time there; however, circumstances did not allow it then. As we enter now, we find a place to sit with other devotees wrapped in devotion.

Although, as a large white man sitting amongst many Indians, I may appear to be different, I do not think there are any in the room who feel greater devotion for this great God-man than I. I am reminded of when Papa Ramdas came to this room and rolled on the floor in ecstasy as the doorman watched in amazement. I am filled with such bliss and inner communion with this great God-man. This time, I drink deeply of the ambrosia of this room, this temple, and acknowledge the heartfelt gratitude I have for the tremendous sadhana Ramakrishna embarked upon while living here and the great realization he attained.

After drinking the bliss-amrita to my heart's content this time, we then wander over to the Panchavati, where Ramakrishna went through great tapasya in order to realize God. This unlettered man from a small village in a remote part of Bengal was the most unlikely personality to become known all over the world and to inspire future generations to lives of seva—self-less service through the Ramakrishna-Vivekananda Mission. Who can understand the vagaries of Grace and where and when a great soul will erupt upon the world scene to change it in such profound ways? It is indeed a mystery that confounds the puny intellect of humankind.

Having had our fill of blessings, we head back to Kolkata to take a little time to digest all that we have received. What joy is ours, what purification we feel, what gifts of Spirit to transmit to one and all! Victory to God, His masters, and to the eternal Light of Spirit!

October 3

4 Gurpar Road—Master's Boyhood Home

Altar in attic room at the boyhood
home of Paramhansa Yogananda.

"Hello! You wait there just one minute. Were you to come at 6 o clock?" The voice comes from the upper balcony of an interior courtyard. We have come to see the childhood home of Mukunda Lal Ghosh, who became the great master, Paramhansa Yogananda. Sarita Ghosh, Master's great niece-in-law, invites us into their home.

As we climb the stairs, each step we take up is a step into the history of our beloved Param-Guru. "Here is the bedroom where Master slept." It is an empty room except for precious pictures lining the wall.

"Look at Lahiri Mahasaya's picture; you can see here his eyes are open." Later, pictures were doctored so that it appears his eyes are shut. To change the picture in this way changes the subtle vibration that comes from the picture and loses the character of the man.

"Just outside this room is where Babaji appeared before Master. He had a great fear about going to the West. Babaji assured him it was all right."

We are guided to another room where, after the death of his mother, Master often slept with his father. Yogananda was for some long time in profound grief after his mother's passing. There are many items belonging to Master: a chair from his childhood, and a table his mother brought as an heirloom from her parents' home—precious items, all.

I explain, we are devotees of Mother Hamilton, and as a point of reference, I tell her that Mother was very good friends with Sister Gyanamata—they were both from Seattle. She goes on to tell a story of Master at the time of Sister Gyanamata's passing from the body.

"Master was out of the ashram at a store with some nuns and monks. Suddenly he said, 'We must go right now, Sister is leaving the body.' When they returned, Gyanamataji was gone. Master touched the top of Sister's head, and it was hot; her feet were cold, but the top of her head was hot. Master explained that when a soul makes a conscious exit from the body, all the energy goes out of the top of the head, and that is why it is hot."

Then we are taken to the attic room where Master meditated. "This is where the Divine Mother and where Krishna appeared to Master. He meditated up here because no one would disturb him up here. At that time, this was the only room on the roof." The room is part of a large complex of family rooms now, a whole new story added since those early times.

She thoughtfully closes the doors to this little attic-meditation room so that we might meditate here for some time in quiet privacy. The room is painted a beautiful color of blue and has an altar of the Kriya Gurus, Swami Kebalananda, Bhaduri Mahasaya (the levitating saint), Master's father, and a beautifully lit picture of Master has been added. Absent from view is the tiger skin of Master's that I sat upon on my previous visit.

Carla and I soon become absorbed in the deep vibrations of Master's Presence. Time and space drop away and there is nothing but pure Spirit. Oh, blessed place, dearest Master, mine. Fathomless glories are revealed, a tiny room with endless space. Jai Guru! No words, no words!

It has been fifteen years since I was last here and Hari Krishna, Master's nephew, gave us a tour of this home; he has since left the body. At that time, I had wished for more time in this attic-meditation room. Tonight, we are given the time to be absorbed in His Light to our heart's content.

Our gracious hosts have been most obliging in opening their home to us. We make an offering and leave some Aplets and Cotlets from Washington State in sincere thankfulness.[10]

Oh Master, thank you for giving your life for us, that we might know God even as you know God. Your legacy has entered the atomic structure of body, mind, and soul. Your rare qualities lift us into heavenly realms where your Spirit constantly abides. You are a bubbling personality of the Infinite, and you are beyond all qualities; you are the eternal Being. May you bless us always with the desire to seek out the same God you found in your little attic room and at the feet of your divine guru. Jai Guru, Jai Gurus.

We take our leave into the darkened night, filled to overflowing from a full day of pilgrimage, radiant with the Master's divine Light.

---

10   A brand name for fruit and nut candies made in Cashmere, Washington, USA.

October 3

BELUR MATH—SAMADHI
TEMPLE OF RAMAKRISHNA

Belur Math Temple.**

We now cross the Hooghly River (a distributary of the Ganges) on the Rabindra Setu, a bridge named for Rabindranath Tagore, the Nobel Laureate. However, the bridge is still commonly called the Howrah Bridge and we are one of 100,000 cars to cross today from Kolkata to Howrah.

From Howrah, we turn upriver and proceed, at a stop-and-go rate, on a very rough road. We are keeping pace alongside children, dressed in blue-and-white school uniforms, being taken to school in bicycle-pulled rickshaws. Each inch of space in traffic is fought for with the intensity of a high-stakes playoff game.

Finally, we come to the large arched gates that tell us we have arrived at Belur Math. This is the site where Swami Vivekananda established an ashram when he returned to India with some Western devotees. It has grown into a large complex that includes Samadhi Temples for Ramakrishna, Sarada Devi (wife of Ramakrishna), Swami Vivekananda, and many of the original disciples of Ramakrishna.

The complex sports a new museum of first-class quality (except for no air conditioning). Referring to a museum in Calcutta, Ramakrishna used the experience as a humorous lesson for keeping the company of saints:

> I visited the museum once. I was shown fossils. A whole animal has become stone! Just see what an effect has been produced by company! Likewise, by constantly living in the company of a holy man, one verily becomes holy.[11]

After our enjoyable tour of the museum, we make our way to the large Samadhi Temple of Ramakrishna. This beautiful structure was inspired by Swami Vivekananda, using motifs from around the world. The motifs were meant to be an all-inclusive message that every religion is seen as a legitimate pathway to God. The architecture was brought into physical reality by the talents of Swami Vijnanananda, a disciple of Ramakrishna who had an engineering background.

We traverse our way to the front of the temple where there sits a life-like statue of Ramakrishna. The vibration of this Temple is charged with spiritual potency; it is felt in the very air. We sit on the marble floor for some time, deeply indrawn into the Master. Released from the things of the world, we sail upon Spiritual

11   Editor's Note: Yogacharya David sourced this quote from elsewhere; it can be found here as well: Wikipedia, sourced from: *American Vedantist,* Issue #74, Summer 2018, Sri Ramakrishna—English Lessons.

wings and feel ourselves transported past the things of time and space. Here, God alone is.

When we feel moved to continue on, we tread up the stairs to Swami Vivekanandaji's room. We peer into his living quarters while standing on the second-floor balcony; a cool breeze from the Ganges is refreshing. Then on to the various samadhi temples built along the river. Sarada Devi, so revered by all the disciples, is highly honored. Swami Vivekananda's Samadhi Temple is powerfully surcharged, even as his personality was while living. It seems there is no end to the blessings that have come to us on this pilgrimage. All according to His will!

We stand in line to get the blessing of Swami Atmasthananda, the current president of the Mission. I had received the darshan of Swami Ranganathananda 15 years ago, when he was the president, and felt so very blessed. Today, I pronam to the swami, and over a little barrier, the current head of the Order throws little candies at me, which makes me laugh when they land in my lap.

On the long bumpy ride back to Kolkata and our hotel suite, we pass by the many preparations for the coming Durga Puja, a huge celebration in West Bengal that will continue for five days. Durga is a manifestation of the Divine Mother. Durga Puja celebrates the victory of the goddess over the evil buffalo-demon Mahishasura—the victory of good over evil. The preparations are extensive, the equivalent of Christmas or Easter in the West. Lights are being hung in the streets; the images of Durga are everywhere, and Prem, our cab driver, tells us, "The streets will be crazy!" An additional meaning was added to this celebration when Durga was identified with the India Independence Movement. We will be gone from the city by the time the celebrations begin and will not experience what it means for these streets to get any crazier than they are on a daily basis!

"O Ram, You have blessed these pilgrims mightily over these past days. Kolkata is difficult, but the pilgrimage feels complete.

Pronams, to You, our dear Lord. Pronams, for Your great blessings. Om Sri Ram Jai Ram Jai Jai Ram!"

We prepare to leave for the holy city of Puri, the setting of Sri
Yukteswar's seaside ashram and Mahasamadhi Temple.

October 7

RAM-ADVENTURES IN KOLKATA AND PURI

Hariharananda's Samadhi Temple, near Puri.

Our stay in Kolkata has been mixed blessings with extreme polarities. The blessings coming from the pilgrimage spots have been of the highest nature, changing us in profound ways. And, we have been challenged to be here, being in a traffic accident (besides some sore muscles, we are ok. The driver was talking on his cell phone when he rear-ended the car in front of us. I told him, "No more cell phone!" He sheepishly agreed). All in all, it is a difficult city energetically and physically.

Even leaving the hotel, the oppositional force was at work. When we arrived at the airport, we realized that a bag had been left at the hotel that had my passport, computer, and other items in it. Three calls to the hotel from the airport finally located the bag, and then 700 rupees (they would take no responsibility for the left bag) for the bag to take a cab ride to the airport for the invaluable contents to be in time for the flight (fortunately, we had left in plenty of time).

Arriving at the airport in Bhubaneswar made a tremendous difference. Psychically, we felt the change from the intense rajasic energy of Kolkata to the relaxed pace of the *City of Temples*. A one-and-a-half-hour cab ride brought us to Puri, where resides the seaside ashram of Sri Yukteswar. Thanks to the internet, we made travel arrangements in advance while in transit from place to place.

India, a place where computer reservations can be made to most anywhere in the country, and cows still wander the roads with abandon! Cell phones are ubiquitous; they have become the way that bills are paid, and most any kind of transaction requires a cell phone as verification of who you are. For instance, if we get Wi-Fi in the hotel, we must enter a cell phone number, and then the pin number is texted to us. No phone, no pin number.

Our hotel sits on a bluff overlooking the ocean. A breeze is gently blowing, but it is still on the hot and humid side. We use the air conditioner in the room, but the feeling here is so different than Kolkata. We arrange for a car and driver to take us to Karar Ashram today. Carla shows the travel agent at the hotel the website for Karar Ashram, which lists its location; he then calls the driver and all is arranged. Only, we are taken to the wrong ashram an hour out of our way from Puri!

The ashram we were taken to was that of Hariharananda. Hariharananda was a direct disciple of Sri Yukteswarji's. He left the body in 2002, having lived many of his last years in Florida, where he had an ashram. The wonderful thing about this "mistaken destination" is that we felt great peace wandering around the temple grounds. The temple is absolutely beautiful, with images of our guru-lineage lining the circular walls. It is wonderful to see Kriya-brethren keeping the Light of the Masters glowing. We walked the grounds and then returned to Puri. Fortunately, as Hariharananda was the owner of Karar Ashram, they were able to give our driver the correct directions to the ashram.

Arriving at Karar Ashram at 11:30 a.m., after our two-hour detour, we read the sign that the ashram closes at 11:30! Oh India, you are the supreme jokester! Directions in India are no easy matter. Even though the ashram had given our driver instructions, we had to stop four times to get clarification on the way. No amount of ringing the doorbell by our driver brings a response. This darshan will need to wait for another day.

Directions in India: there are no grids for addresses in India; there is no 300 block, 400 block, etc., no proper (by Western standards) ways to find an address. Quite commonly, an address will incorporate landmarks, such as "near the college," or "just behind the oak tree," as a means of helping the seeker of an address. Perhaps one day GPS coordinates will be incorporated into an address to make things easier. Our watchword here is, "verify three times"—this does not guarantee success, but it helps it along!

The adventure continues. We will go to Sri Yukteswar's Karar Ashram tomorrow. We also plan to get a close-up view of the famous Jagannath Temple; as non-Hindus are not allowed in, we will view it from a nearby building.

The location of the Golden Sands (Sterling Holidays) Hotel where we are staying is wonderful. We are outside of town; in fact, it is a very bumpy dirt road with mud puddles the size of small ponds on the way to get here. So, it is far away from the noise and the dense packing of hotels along the beach in town. With a beautiful view of the ocean and a pristine swimming pool, it has been a welcome respite from Delhi and Calcutta.

We have very limited use of the office computer for internet, but the food is good. We have gone to skipping dinner in favor of a protein/greens drink. The cost is about $40 a night; this includes a breakfast buffet. There are no bugs; there is a steady breeze from the ocean, and the temperature, humidity, and beauty remind me of the coast of Mexico. There are many religious paintings/icons in the hotel, which help give a feeling of something more than pure materialism, and the staff is excellent, although English is spoken by a very few.

The hotel has hired some artists to create traditional murals on the entry to the hotel. We watch them work, drawing and painting largely freehand, but with incredible precision. It is wonderful to see artists who are masters of their craft at work.

Tomorrow we are determined to make it to Karar Ashram and the famous Jagannath Temple.

October 7

JAGANNATH TEMPLE

Jagannath Temple central tower.

Today we start with a new driver, but he knows Mannu, our driver from yesterday, so I ask him to call Mannu to get directions, and he now knows the way. We first proceed to Jagannath Temple. Cars are not allowed to proceed closer than one-half of a kilometer from the Temple, so we hire a bicycle rickshaw; we are cautious of the heat and sun, as Carla was over-come with heat when we were walking back from the Taj Mahal.

Our rider/driver takes us down to the Temple. The library, from which most days you can get a glimpse of the Temple from the outside, is closed today. He offers to take us around the perimeter of the Temple, which we agree to (all of this is done without a common word language, but we seem to get on all right without words).

Jagannath means "Lord of the Universe," and the Temple is part of the holy Char Dham pilgrimage. It is one of four sites, the others being: Badrinath, Dwarka, and Rameswaram, representing the four cardinal points of India. It is a pilgrimage particularly of interest to worshipers of Krishna and Vishnu (Krishna is a manifestation of Vishnu).

We feel a definite spiritual power emanating from this Temple. Non-Hindus are not allowed entry; even foreigners who claim to be Hindu are prohibited. Similar to Judaism, Hindus are not interested in converts, for much emphasis is placed on genetic lineage.

Our driver deposits us on a filthy lane where another man eagerly guides us through a narrow maze between buildings that are living quarters for families. Truly, the subsistence level of so many Indians is meager. We emerge through some three-stories of steps, where trash is swept out of the way as we ascend uncertain steps, and finally, we emerge onto the flat rooftop that has a view from the side of the Temple complex.

Ancient towers and gardens abound across the street from our rooftop view. Amidst the garbage and scantily clad children with us, we feel a wonderful Shakti emanating from this Temple. Perhaps these children are physically impoverished, but they live in a spiritually-charged environment. Who can tell who is impoverished and who is wealthy in comparison? Of course, the golden middle path would point in the direction of having a balance of both physical and spiritual health and prosperity as the ideal.

Carla stands rooted in place, absorbed in these environments. As has happened on several occasions on this pilgrimage, she has been deeply affected. When we went to Master's boyhood home, she burst into uncontrolled tears. For the sincere aspirant, pilgrimage destinations can have a profound effect beyond the conscious mind's understanding. We feel greatly uplifted from our viewpoint of this holy site.

We circumambulate the Temple clockwise on the streets; our very sweet rickshaw driver returns us to our car and driver. He asks for no extra money, but I quadruple his rate and he is all smiles. Somehow, I feel such great love for this bicycle rickshaw driver, communicating on a level beyond words, feeling it deeply in the Soul. God bless his heart.

October 7

Karar Ashram

Yogacharya David at Sri Yukteswar's Samadhi Temple.

With the landmark "Sky Hotel" clearly in mind, we turn into a narrow alleyway and drive down the length of a football field or so, take the second left onto an even more narrow drive, and from here, we can see the yellow sign for Karar Ashram.

At last, the proper time and place have come together, but what is this? Three or four minutes of ringing the bell bring no response, but at last an older man makes his way to the gate. It is a strange little gate; the narrow door opens inward and immediately you are surrounded by a gated area that requires you to close the door before you are able to move into the grounds.

Our host speaks little English, but nevertheless speaks quite freely as he guides us to the meditation hall; never mind that we do not understand a single word he is saying. In the meditation hall, we are allowed to peruse the pictures on the walls; one picture is missing from my time here before, a picture of Sri Yukteswar taken after his Mahasamadhi.

He then walks us to the Samadhi Temple. Master came up with the general design and Sananda Lal Ghosh, Master's artist-brother, drew up the plans. He unlocks the doors and leads us into the small mandir. He proudly indicates that it is he who keeps the temple and that all the plastic flowers adorning the place are his invention.

We ask to sit in meditation; he indicates only a short time is allowed. We sit, feeling the power of Sri Yukteswar's Presence. Perhaps after ten minutes, the attendant returns to close up the Samadhi Temple. It is for this Temple I have come and that I have been interested in Carla coming to experience; I do not feel complete with our time.

A verbal tussle ensues, in which I inform the attendant that this is "not correct," and we should be allowed more time. Meanwhile, he is locking the place up. As we walk away, I continue to strongly put forth our case. He replies in a few words of English and mostly his native tongue that the ashram Swami has made the rules and he is helpless to change them. I was just reading a biography of Sri Yukteswarji and his rebellion against senseless rules and feel his blessing to do battle here.

Then suddenly, Carla Ma enters the fray. She says that we have come from the USA for this purpose only, and suddenly the tide changes. He relents and opens the mandir once again, and indicates that if anyone else comes, then we need to vacate the Temple. We agree and he goes off.

We are given another half-hour here, being absorbed in the presence and the power of the master. Fifteen years previous, I had felt the master's joy; today, I feel his power. Toward the end, we are feeling complete. Whatever was to be transferred has been accomplished and I feel ready to go. Just at that time, the attendant returns with some other guest in tow; with gratitude, we pronam to him. Sri Yukteswarji made us fight for him, but he also acquiesced. Jai Gurus, Jai Swami Sri Yukteswarji.

Our attendant seems to have undergone some change since we arrived. Whereas he was grudging before, now he is all courtesy. I ask about Sri Yukteswar's bedroom, and he tells us that the Swami, who is not here, has the only key to that room. On my previous visit, we had been given access to this room by the Swami, and it was powerful to be in that room.

However, today, our attendant offers to open a small room adjacent to Sri Yukteswar's bedroom that I had not seen before. He says this was Sri Yukteswar's puja room. There is barely room enough for Carla and me to be in this room at the same time. In the front is a picture of the fierce Kali Ma and next to it, our guide tells us, is Sri Yukteswar's original picture of Lahiri Mahasaya. There are other pictures of all the masters, and small statues of them as well.

This room is powerful; a sweet uplifting feeling is truly here. This "bonus room" is really a gift. I feel great gratitude for the transformation of our guide and his opening of this room for us. Perhaps he somehow saw that we were not casual tourists, but devotees of the master, and this opened his heart.

Oh Lord, Oh Sri Yukteswarji, "You may challenge us to remain steadfast in our quest, you may not open the doors straight away, but when your heart is touched, then *all the doors do open themselves, all the lights do light themselves, darkness like a dark bird flies away, oh flies away!*"

Thank you, our dear Master, our beloved Param-param Guru.

October 8

SHRIYUKTESWAR'S MAHASAMADHI

Picture of Shriyukteswar from
Hariharananda's Ashram.

found this a fascinating description of Shriyukteswar's
Mahasamadhi, and I thought you would find it inspiring as well.

Excerpted from *Swami Shriyukteshwar: Incarnation of Wisdom*
by Paramahansa Prajnanananda

Beginning of the End

It was March 9th, 1936, a Monday afternoon. In the Karar
Ashram at Puri, Swami Shriyukteshwar called out to his
disciple, a young monk, "Narayan! Narayan!" Narayan,

who was always present at the feet of his master, came to him. Shriyukteshwar declared, "It is my time to depart from the world, Narayan! Today, I will leave this body! Hearing this Narayan was greatly disturbed and could not control his sorrow. Shriyukteshwar repeated, "Can you get me a glass of water?" Narayan quickly brought a glass of water, but as he gave it to the master, it fell down on the floor.

Shriyukteshwar remarked, "Have you noticed how I am being separated from you Narayan? But do not be upset. Your love, service, and devotion to the guru are beyond comparison. I was very contented with your service. Our relationship is truly eternal."

Dusk fell and the day was about to pass. The sun was setting. Shriyukteshwar called upon a person named Krutivasa and said, "Krutivasa! Immediately go to Puri railway station and ask Prabhasa to inform Yogananda, who is now in Calcutta, that I am leaving my body this evening. He can come to Puri by the night train. It is my time to depart." (Prabhas Ghosh was a cousin brother of Paramahansa Yogananda and an executive officer in the railway department. In those days, there were no direct telephone connections and messages had to be sent from station to station. As soon as Prabhas at Kharagpur received the message, he informed Paramahansa Yogananda and also made all arrangements for his journey to Puri that night.) But Yoganandaji was not informed about the declaration of Shriyukteshwar of leaving his body.

Sitting on a small bed in lotus posture, Shriyukteshwar asked Narayan to hold his chest and back with two hands. Narayan followed the master's direction. The great master and yogi went into deep meditation. His body seemed calm and sedate. A mild vibration passed from his heart to the fontanel, producing a divine sound resembling the "Om" sound. As that sound merged into the cosmic sound, the great master left his gross body, and the body became a little stiff. Not noticing this, Narayan continued his massage.

In the meantime, Krutibasa returned from the railway station. Swami Narayan asked him to sit near the master and himself went to fetch a doctor disciple by the name of Dr. Dinakar Rao, who lived next door, to examine the master. After a thorough examination, the doctor declared that the master must have left his body about a half hour earlier.

Swami Narayan stood motionless in great despair with tears rolling down his face. "Oh, Great Master," he sobbed, "Your play on this earth was remarkable. Whoever came into contact with you was fascinated by you and was transformed by your divinity and boundless eternal wisdom. Your tall body, long arms, wide forehead, and strong chest, your bright, star-like eyes, always in sambhavi mudra, and your tranquil bearded face live on forever in the hearts of all who had the privilege of meeting you."

The divine child born in Serampore on the banks of river Ganga ended his physical existence of 81 years by Puri by the seaside. But his teachings live on in the hearts of millions of spiritual seekers all around the world.[12]

---

12   *Swami Sriyukteshwar: Incarnation of Wisdom.* Foreword.

October 9

DHAULI HILL

Dhauli Hill Peace Stupa.

A n hour-and-a-half taxi ride from Puri brings us to the boundary of Bhubaneswar, "India's Temple City." Located in the state of Odisha (formerly Orissa), it has apparent prosperity with a vast array of building projects as new industry has grown. I was drawn to come here because of the Udayagiri (Sunrise Hill) caves that date back to the time before Christ, built for Jain ascetics.

Before we get to the Udayagiri caves, we are directed by the hotel travel agent to go see Dhauli Hills. It was in this area that King Ashoka (304–232 BCE) fought the Kalinga War. The king was devastated at the terrible cost of the battle that "made the Daya

River turn red" with the blood of 100,000 killed. King Ashoka went on to be a proponent of Buddhism and social precepts that would serve as a cultural foundation for political unity. King Ashok ruled most of what is today India, into Pakistan and Bangladesh.

Thousands of pillars were created that stretched as far as the Mediterranean Sea that spoke of Ashoka's thoughts on Buddha's teachings. It was during his reign that many of the important locations of the Buddha's life were identified.

H.G. Wells wrote of King Ashoka in his book, *The Outline of History*:

> Amidst the tens of thousands of names of monarchs that crowd the columns of history, their majesties and graciousnesses and serenities and royal highnesses and the like, the name of Asoka shines, and shines, almost alone, a star.[13]

On our way up the hill, there are stone carvings with edicts from King Ashoka and his concern for the whole world; he looked to replace brute force with the power of dharma, knowing that there must be a better way to live than mass killings through war.

As we continue our ascent, we come into view of a shining white dome that marks the site of the Peace Stupa (Stupa being a mound that contains the remains of Buddhist monks). We view wonderful stone reliefs that depict various aspects of the Buddha's life. There are wide vistas from the hilltop, including looking down on the Daya River that had one day run red and made a lasting impression on the ruler of India—that event helped change the world.

This Peace Stupa or Pagoda was the inspiration of a Japanese Buddhist, Fuji Guruji, who came to India in 1930 to help Mahatma

---

13   *The Outline of History* by H.G. Wells (p. 322).

Gandhiji in his non-violent movement. Later Fuji Guruji inspired a Peace Stupa in Bihar State, and that led the governor Sri Nityananda Kanungo to establish a Peace Stupa here in his homeland of Odisha. This Peace Pagoda stands on a prominent hill as a message to the world to refrain from war and violence and to be a beacon of peace for one and all.

October 9

UDAYAGIRI CAVES

Raninka Na'ara: Queen's Palace Cave 1, Udayagiri, Odisha.

A s we enter the gate to the manicured grounds of the Udayagiri Caves, there is an intense verbal fight occurring between a large man in a blue shirt and the guard at the gate. The large man is shouting furiously at the guard who is remaining cool during the verbal assault. This tirade continues on and on, for at least five minutes, without the large man gaining satisfaction or the guard losing his reserve. Oh, Ram! What an interesting way you have introduced us to these caves of silence and meditation!

After Buddhism was ascendant here in Odisha, the Jains became the most powerful movement in the second and first centuries before Christ; it was for these Jain ascetics that these caves were made. After the Jains, the Hindus gained ascendency, then later the Muslims: afterward, it was the British, and for the last sixty years, it has been self-rule. Hundreds, even thousands, of years can see a dominant religion, school of thought, or political system reign supreme, but eventually, each has a spent life, a beginning, middle, and end. It all goes to show there is no permanency on this earth.

The only lasting theme in human history is God-experience; this alone survives down the ages. It has various guises and forms, but the essential nature of it remains the same and can be identified by one who has had that same universal transformation.

I have felt a magnetic draw to these ancient caves; we have arrived for the purpose of finding traces of the divine vibrations left as a lasting signature of the spiritual work accomplished here. The fame and park-like setting of the caves have made this as much a tourist attraction as a pilgrimage site. I have found this to be the case in places both East and West.

When I was at Kanyakumari at the south point of India, where Swami Vivekananda meditated and had a profound vision, there was no place to meditate, and the police with whistles moved the crowds through without a moment to take in the nature of the place! There are no whistling police officers here, and it is not so crowded, but most are here to see a sight.

We wander the beautifully sculptured caves in peace and find many wonderful caves in which to sit and feel the substrata of spiritual vibration that continues to reverberate here. It is tremendously hot and humid on this midday journey, but we are happy to be in the relatively cool and dry caves. These caves are very fine: smooth floors and delightful carvings.

Climbing to the top of the hill, there is a breeze that is cooling. I wander down a trail behind the main caves. We go down into a grove of interesting trees and there is a distinct change. Oh, this is powerful; a tremendous event happened here, a great Soul achieved mahasamadhi bliss. Time dissolves; there is no time, only the beginningless, endless Existence. A potent stillness pervades this grove and it has called me to itself. This is what drew me; this is a tremendous Soul who gained a remarkable realization and left the body here so long ago. We remain here for some time, both of us drinking in the salient feeling.

We depart from this sacred grove and delight in elephant sculptures and other caves, each one wonderful. However, the magnet that drew me is the grove and those who have inhabited this place. There is no marker here as there are for the caves; it remains a secret grove of heavenly proportions that would not fit easily into a tour guide's book.

Upon our departure, the angry man is gone. I wish the big angry man peace. He may have had a righteous cause; however, it was misplaced upon the poor guard at the gate. And may the guard be blessed for remaining cool under fire. Om Sri Ram Jai Ram Jai Jai Ram! Despite the initial disturbance, these caves and the sacred grove have been a blessing for us.

October 13

Swami Vishwananda

Yogacharya David with Swami Vishwananda.

"Hari Om, Namaskar!" There stands Swami Vishwananda at the gate of his home, welcoming us. It is a great joy to see Swamiji, it has been eight years since we have seen him last. After he gives me a hug, I take his hand, for his steps are less than steady, although he displays a strong grip.

Swamiji is now 94 years old and it shows physically, although he, in all other ways, is as vigorous and full of life as ever! We enter his apartment. He has shifted since we were last here. He is now on the ground floor. Stairs are not possible for him to manage. The room that Rama Mani occupied is now kept as a shrine, with pictures of the saints she knew and loved, and who loved her, carefully kept in place.

"Yes, I miss her," Swamiji admits, choking up as he speaks of his beloved niece. "She was loved by so many saints, Ma always treated her special, Papa always asked her to sing, and Shankaracharya would always give her special attention."

We miss her quiet presence and her care of Swamiji. His quarters are not as well kept as when she did her immaculate service, and her stuffed aloo parathas are still the best I have ever tasted.

Swamiji immediately launches into a clear remembrance of our circumambulation of India in 1998. He recalls in particular our journey to Puttaparthi.

"You became aware of one area, and said you felt the presence of great souls there. Madam (speaking to Carla), there is a bathing tank there on that hill, and very great souls have meditated there. He (David) was somehow knowing of that! I have spent time there, thirty days, fourteen days, a wonderful place." Memories poured forth from Swamiji like a river constantly flowing.

"One thing sir, you must go to Kanyakumari. One Swami Vivekananda meditated on that rock. When Vivekananda arrived there he immediately dove into those waters and swam to the rock. I went there myself. When I arrived I too dove in and swam. The boatman there was very excited (disturbed) that I was swimming in those waters, but I went over. There was no Temple there at that time."

I had not heard this particular from Swamiji before. I have written about being at Kanyakumari in *My Spiritual India*. The story goes that when Swami Vivekananda arrived at Kanyakumari as a wandering mendicant, he asked a boatman for a ride to those distant rocks. The boatman asked for money, but since Vivekananda carried none with him, he immediately dove into the ocean and swam to the rocks. The shocked boatman could not believe this Swami was braving those shark-infested waters; he told other villagers about this bold stroke. Many of the villagers then rowed out to the island and begged Swamiji his forgiveness and offered him food and water, which he refused. He was determined to spend time meditating there in order to get clarity on his life's mission. Swami Vishwananda had bravely followed in swimming over as well; not an easy feat!

Swamiji expressed great concern over the current course of India, that people were losing their way. "I have seen it! Before there was correct behavior. Now, so much materialism and corruption." He went on at length. I too worry that India keeps her spiritual bearings while navigating in modern technological waters.

Abhay and his wife, Lalitha, arrive and bring lunch with them. I ask Abhay to relate a story he told me previously of when Hanuman blessed him, which I record on video along with stories Swamiji is relating as well.

I feel great bliss being with Swami Vishwananda. He said that yesterday he had been quite dull, but today he is full of life, vigor, every inch the force of nature that we have always known him to be. He claims it is due to me, but I know that he has led a dynamic life and it is such a joy to share this time with him. His depth of spirituality is wonderful, like a beautiful patina that increasingly glows with luster through time.

Swamiji has been intimate with some of the great spiritual personalities of his time: Anandamayi Ma (she is his Guru), Ramana Maharshi, Papa Ramdas, Shankarcharya, Anandashram Swami, Maharishi Mahesh Yogi, Satya Sai Baba, and many others. He has moved in high circles, such as when the President of India asked Swamiji to organize a private audience with the Shankarcharya, which he did. Anandamayi Ma also asked Swamiji to arrange to see the Shankaracharya.

Swamiji went on to say, apparently there is some talk of it, that Satya Sai Baba was gradually poisoned, murdered due to the vast wealth that surrounded him. India is nothing if not rife with rumors, and certainly spiritual personalities, especially famous and rich ones, are subject to every speculation, true and not true.

Swamiji went on, with a little prompting to relate stories from the Mahabharata. I sat in a blissful state as he proceeded from story to story, treasuring my time with this special soul.

When we take our leave, he sees us out to the street and helps us give directions to the autorickshaw driver. He is the picture of love and good will, a rare soul whose fire still burns bright. Pronams, Swamiji.

October 14

ARRIVAL AT ANANDASHRAM, ABODE OF BLISS

Swami Satchidananda; background, Swami Ramdas.

W e are seven minutes before six p.m., riding in the car from the Mangalore airport. I had wanted to be at the ashram before six in order to be in time for the closing of the Mandir. I know about where we are as we crest a hill before descending the back way to the ashram and I do not see any possible way, according to laws of physics, that we can be there before six.

"Oh Papa, You know what is in my heart; time and space are Your playthings. If it be Thy will, bend time and allow us, Your children, to arrive in time for the Mandir Closing." Somehow, and the only explanation in my mind is that Papa did bend time and space, we arrived a few minutes before six.

> Oh Papa, You have rulership over this entire universe. Even the slightest desires of your dear ones can elicit a response from Your almighty will. Teach us to rely upon Divine Will alone, cheerfully submitting to what You decide that is for our highest good." Carla and I enter the Swamiji's Mandir from opposite sides.
>
> Oh my Lord, this is like coming home. All voices joined in joyful unison singing Your name. We feel wrapped in a spiritual warmth that unifies all here. Something inside stirs, such a deep familiarity. It is true I have spent time here over the years, however this sense of connectedness transcends a single lifetime's depth of experience.

Such a warm greeting from Swami Muktananda, Sri Krishna, Anantraman, Swami Chandrananada, who was a newly minted Swami last time we were here, Saint Nalini, and too many to name. My heart overflows with Divine Love, swimming in a sea of smiles, love, and joy. "How long has it been?" We are asked. "Seven years? Oh, it cannot be so long!"

We take our room in #4 of Ramdas block. The ashram is filled to overflowing; there are two groups here. One group is made up of devotees of Meher Baba; they have a continuous chanting program for 48 hours. The group, complete with a loudspeaker, are directly above us on what used to be the rooftop, but a canopy was built a few years ago so it is now covered. Another group is chanting *Hari Rama, Hari Krishna* for seven days without a break in the Centenary Hall. Our dear friend Chandra has been participating in this and is very uplifted from the experience.

It is insisted that we take our meals in our room for the next few days as the canteen is very full. Lakshmi Mahadev comes to

our room. "Oh I have only recently been informed of your coming, I will be going away next day after (day after tomorrow), I am
so very sorry." However, she is glad to hear we will be here for
some time and we will see her when she returns.

The power then goes out. A quick search produces some
"torches" from our luggage. A knock at the door and Saint Nalini
brings a candle and one match. "We have had so much rain this
year that this is the only match I could find that would light!"
Minutes later Anantraman comes and brings another candle. So
much love and concern for our slightest comfort.

We enter the Bhajan Hall. There sits Papa and Mataji in their
life-like poses in front, and now there is the addition of Swami
Satchidananda's form. This is my first time back to Anandashram
since his Mahasamadhi. I pronam when I enter and then I seat
myself up close to Swamiji's picture, my back to the arched wall.

When it seems the right moment, I go into Papa's small room;
it is the original part of this now-larger structure that once served
as Papa's only room along with a covered porch. I pronam to the
altar, and then I proceed to Papa's, Mataji's, and then Swamiji's
realistic paintings that are on hard board that is cut to match the
outline of their physical bodies, making them appear so life-like
sitting there.

When I reach Swamiji's picture, a tide of emotion rises up.
There is no single emotion; there is some feeling of loss, and there
is gratitude, love; so many emotions are there, not any one single
thing but a combination of all. Even as I write this, I feel it, and yet
there is nothing distinct I can say about this floodtide. Tears flow
freely from the eyes.

I truly cannot say it is a feeling of loss, for I feel his thoughts
and presence with me. His picture does not seem an ordinary
picture, but a living Presence.

Oh, my dear Swamiji, You have been so instrumental in what I have in God. I have often referred to You as my second Mother, Mother Hamilton being my first Mother. With unbounded love and perseverance, you helped to chip away the dross that covered the Divine Light within this "temple not made with hands." My love and gratitude are endless, and I surrender myself to your holy feet. Om Sri Ram Jai Ram Jai Jai Ram.

It was this holy Nam that you chanted for your final realization. It was this all-powerful chant my own Gurudev initiated me into almost 40 years ago.

Om Sri Ram Jai Ram Jai Jai Ram: Victory to God, Victory to the Light for this entire world. Your pure Light is radiating through so many souls here. What a rare thing to have such continuous illumined masters in this lineage, Papa, Mataji, and You, my dear Swamiji. May this ashram ever be a beacon of purity and Light for one and all. Om Sri Ram Jai Ram Jai Jai Ram!

We end the evening program with the aarti as once again the singing joins us together and brings such brotherhood. Kannan rushes across the Bhajan Hall for pronam greetings. He appears to have had some health issues; he says he was not well last year but he is all right now.

Our hearts are quite full with all the love we have been greeted with. Arriving on time for the closing of the Mandir, being enfolded in the loving vibrations of singing the Holy Name, receiving Prasad under a tropical night sky, and sitting in warm comfort with a half-moon hanging overhead is all pure bliss.

Oh Papa, Mataji, Swamiji, due to your committed lives for God and Gurus, alone you have created this abode of bliss. May we, with your blessings, bring this light, love, and purity to all with whom we come into contact. Our fervent prayer is that all may experience the Divine Union that was your all, and all, in all.

Let the name of God ring from hills and dales and in the hearts of all, by whatever Name each one chooses to sing with love and faith. Om Sri Ram Jai Ram Jai Jai Ram!

October 14

PRAYERS FOR PURI

Garuda, the eagle who carries
Vishnu; this statue sits prominently
between the hotel and the sea at Puri.

A powerful typhoon just hit Puri. We loved out time in Puri and the people there.

We were there a week ago. Please pray for the residents to be safe, and that all should keep their mind on God. It is a holy city. May God protect it.

These past few days, Puri has been in the news as it has taken the brunt of a typhoon (in the Atlantic, it is called a hurricane). Just six days ago, we were there in a hotel looking out over the beach and vast water. It must be quite a difficult thing to go through for all there; in fact, they have evacuated many people from the area.

The hotel we stayed at had a lobby that had no walls on two sides. The restaurant was also open like that. Those winds and rains must be lashing through the hotel at incredible speeds and power. Those who are there are no strangers, but friends.

In fact, how can we say that any in the world are strangers? Are not all our intimates? If there is suffering by anyone, is it not our very self that is also suffering? This universal empathy would not be possible without the Presence of God in the midst, for it would overwhelm the individual mind. However, the universal mind of God can easily accommodate this expansion.

Even as you might say, "Oh, I just stubbed my toe, ouch!" And then later you notice, "Oh, that food tastes so good!" And all through the day you are aware of so many different parts of your body relating experiences to your mind.

Now, your toe might be thinking, "I have nothing to do with those tastes in the mouth." And the mouth may say, "I have nothing to do with that lowly toe!" However, the brain sees it all as part of the same body. Even so, God sees all parts of creation as His very self, and there is no part that is separate or dispensable.

May those souls in Puri be safe, and may the damage from the storm result in even better buildings through their restoration. Om Sri Ram Jai Ram Jai Jai Ram.

October 17

SWAMI CHIDANANDA PURI: "YOU AND I ARE DOING THE SAME WORK."

Swami Chidananda Puri, India.

We enter into what had been Swami Satchidananda's receiving room and is now Swami Muktananda's. This brings back such memories. I seek out "my place" on the floor where I sat so many years ago in front of Swami Satchidananda, but Sri Krishna insists that I take a chair he has placed near Swamiji.

At one point, a swami enters in and takes pronam from Swami Muktananda. The swami exits; what was said was not in English. Swami Muktananda then tells me that a great saint and scholar, one Swami Chidananda Puri, is just now coming. I comment that not all scholars are saints, so this swami is a rarity. Swami Muktananda agrees. He says he is very active and in charge of many projects going on all over the place, that he travels extensively.

We wait for a few minutes and a swami, perhaps in his fifties, enters in at a fast clip and sits in the chair provided. There is a rapid exchange between the two swamis as the room fills up with various devotees; their dialogue is not in English.

This lack of verbal understanding gives me plenty of opportunity to observe the man introduced as a Saint and a scholar. He is, of course, dressed in orange. He is bearded, has short cropped hair but not shaved, and he has a solid white strip across his forehead that extends into his hair from front to back along the crown, denoting Shiva. He has a pleasing manner, can be quick moving but is not fidgety. Swami Muktananda, Swami Chidananda and I are seated in a triangle.

After some minutes, I can tell Swami Muktananda is saying something about me that includes "Yogananda Paramhansa." The swami turns his attention to me as Swami Muktananda has gone out for a moment. "You are from where?" "USA." "I am from near Calicut." Then the swami looks at me. I feel the power and Light of God spontaneously rise up in me as I hold his gaze. His demeanor changes as now he looks at me with unblinking eyes. Then his eyes shift upward above my head; he is seeing something about my nature.

Swami Muktananda reenters and the two swamis return to their talk. Swami Muktananda is explaining about how some of the ashram projects are proceeding. Then the Swami Chidananda looks at me again with a clear gaze. He says, "You do the same work as I do." I said, "I am just a little person, like a small child." Others laugh, he smiles, but does not say anything.

After some more talk between he and Swami Muktananda he stands to walk out. We all stand with him; as he is nearby, I reach down and touch his feet. He draws me up and is smiling and laughing, filled with joy he gives me a hug. Then, with full-on directness he says, "You do the same work as I do." I take this as his blessing, for he is a saint who knows God.

October 20

SWAMI SATCHIDANANDA'S LAST FOUR YEARS AND MAHASAMADHI

Swami Satchidananda, 2007.

We are sitting in satsang. It is Swami Muktananda, Swami Chandrananda, Carla and me. I ask Swami Muktananda, "Can you please tell me about Swami Satchidananda's passing?" Swamiji's appearance is solemn, then he says:

> Yes. At one time, the year is 2003, Swamiji said, "I am leaving on December 3rd." We could not believe what he was saying. Later on, we asked him, "Swamiji, did we hear you

right, are you going to leave the body on December 3rd?"
He said, "Yes."

Eventually December 3rd came and we were all quite
anxious. At the end of the day, Swamiji said, so childlike
[Swami Muktananda and Swami Chandrananda are laugh-
ing], "Well (waving of the hand back and forth), nothing
has happened!" [We all laughed].

Then, March or April, 2004, Swamiji was having so
much angina pain. For proper treatment, the doctors
all said that Swamiji should be taken to Mangalore. This
could be Swamiji's decision only, so we asked. Swamiji
said, "I do not wish to go, but Papa says I should." So, he
was taken. So many doctors were consulted and he was
taking medicines, but the pain was intense. It was decided
that Swamiji should have angioplasty. Swamiji said yes to
the procedure, "The pain is so intense it is no use going
on like this." [long pause, there were several long pauses
in the telling, at times Swami Muktananda had a lot of
emotion while relating these events.]

The procedure was done, and at first it appeared
that everything was alright. Then someone noticed that
Swamiji had no movement on one side of his body. The
doctors said Swamiji has had a stroke. (Long pause)

Afterwards Swamiji was brought back to the ashram.
He very much wanted to walk again. There was physical therapy; he did everything to be able to walk. But, so
many times when he tried to walk, the angina pain would
stop it.

Swamiji suffered so much for four and a half years. So
much, nobody knows. Toward the end we knew that the
end was near. Body functions were shutting down.

Nalini related at another time: "The window at the
Centenary Hall was open and all were in the main room

chanting Ram Nam. For a long time the chanting was for his recovery. However, Swamiji was in such great pain that we no longer chanted for his life to continue, not for the way things were."

Swamiji's 13th Day Service is described in a later posting, "Satsang with Swami Muktananda."

October 20

SATSANG WITH SWAMI MUKTANANDAJI

Yogacharya David and Swami Muktananda.

After discussing with Swami Muktananda about publishing the Ashram Books on Amazon and the showing of *Mystic India*, which we have brought with us, we moved on to our favorite subject, Swami Satchidananda. (This narrative reflects the free-flowing conversation that we had.)

Swami Muktananda: "Have you gone to Papa's Cave where he had the vision of Jesus?"

David: "No, we tried on two occasions, but both times, Papa did not allow us to go."

Swami Muktananda continued:

We have been. With this last flood of the Ganges, the cave was severely damaged. When Swami Shuddhananda left the body, Swami Chidananda told us that we should have a traditional ceremony 13 days after his passing. You see, with Papa and Mataji we had something on the 13th day, 9 or 10 thousand people came on each occasion. But, we did not do it in the traditional way. Papa did not want traditions observed for his passing. He was cremated instead of buried in salt and other items in the lotus posture as swamis often times are. When Chidananda said we should observe tradition with Swami Shuddhananda, we felt it was Papa's will.

When Swami Satchidananda left the body, we asked him before if we should observe tradition with him, he said that since we did with Swami Shuddhananda he felt it was Papa's will that we should continue.

We invited so many sadhus from all over Kerala. We had five or six hundred sadhus; each were provided with 32 items; we washed each one of their feet, fed them, and gave them some money. It was raining so hard every day beforehand; we put up tents in the Panchavati and over by the Sadhudham. Then, on the day, it did not rain all day until 6 o'clock and everything was done.

We hired a professional cook to handle the food. We told him to prepare for three or four thousand people; we had seven thousand at least! We were running out of food and someone suggested we send to one of the vegetarian hotels for food. We did so and that made the difference. We were not going to allow anyone to go away hungry!

So, for Swamiji's 13th day, we did everything traditionally. When Swami Chidananda passed away, our Swami was not feeling well. We are so closely connected with Shivananda Ashram, but I did not know whether to go because things were serious here. I told them, make arrangements for it, but I will not decide now.

It was just a day before, and I decided I could go there. It was very tight planning but I arrived on time. Swami Chidananda had asked to be bodily dropped into the Ganges near Rishikesh. He was taken out in a boat and slowly, slowly let down into the water. They tied some stones (to his body) so that he would not float to the surface.

Afterward I had a couple of hours and went to the cave where Papa had the vision of Jesus and I spent a couple of hours there. The feeling there (long pause), so calm, peaceful! I cannot describe.

Swami Muktananda then pulled up on his computer a writing from Swami Chinmayananda (the same teacher as Lakshmi Mahadevi had). The writing was a transcription of the Swami speaking about the Mahasamadhis of Swami Shivananda and Papa Ramdas. He talked about them as being the two lights of India. This talk of Chinmayananda was in Chennai.

Swami Muktananda, after he read from Chinmayananda, stated, "I was there when he said this. I may have heard of Papa before, but I became interested in him from what Chinmayananda said. I first came to the ashram in 1963."

As we were talking, the time came for the closing of the Mandir. Swami Muktananda said, "Hari Om!" We took our leave with gratitude in our hearts for all the first-hand descriptions and uplifting talks about Saints and their lives. Om Sri Ram Jai Ram Jai Jai Ram.

October 26

CHRISTINE BALDIGARA'S PASSAGE

Christine's photo on altar in
Master's meditation room, Calcutta.

little before midnight, the phone rang; it was Angela calling to say her mother breathed her last about a half hour
before (it was Thursday, October 24th in late morning
there).

The way that Christine passed is inspiring and conveys the
nature of her soul. The day before her passing, we spoke to
Christine; the phone was put to her ear. As I was telling her the
masters' presence was with her, she said, "Yes." Then when Carla
was speaking to her, saying Om Sri Ram, Christine then held
the phone in both hands (a surprise to everyone) and said, "Om
Sri Ram."

After the phone conversation, George led everyone in singing Ram Nam, accompanied by Andrea, Angela and Honor while sitting with Christine. The next morning, Angela and Andrea came to see Christine and when they walked in, Christine was repeating Ram Nam. Andrea put some ice to Christine's lips and afterwards she repeated Om, Om, Om. From that moment her breathing changed, which the nurse identified as the final breaths; she left the body chanting Om.

From a spiritual viewpoint, this is a supreme way to leave the body achieved by the greatest of devotees. In *The Bhagavad Gita,* Krishna tells Arjuna:

> And, in the hour when life is ending,
> With mind set fast and in trustful piety,
> Drawing still breath beneath calm brows unbending,
> In happy peace that faithful one doth die,
> In glad peace passeth to Purusha's heaven.
> The place which they who read the Vedas name
> Aksharam, "Ultimate," whereto have striven
> Saints and ascetics—their road is the same.
> That way—the highest way—goes he who shuts
> The gates of all his senses, locks desire
> Safe in his heart, centres the vital airs
> Upon his parting thought, steadfastly set;
> And, murmuring OM, the sacred syllable—
> Emblem of BRAHM—dies, meditating on Me.
> For who, none other Gods regarding, looks
> Ever to Me, easily am I gained
> By such a Yogi[ni]; and, attaining me,
> They fall not—those Mahatmas—back to birth,
> To life, which is the place of pain, which ends,
> But take the way of utmost blessedness.[14]

---

14   *Bhagavad Gita* (Chapter 8).

So, we are assured that Christine ascended directly to God and the Masters. And what great joy that brings to the Masters when a soul leaves the body in such a way. After Christine's passing, George again led all in singing Ram Nam. Truly, a blessed passing.

Please keep the family and all loved ones in your thoughts and prayers, that all may feel the great Comforter and inner assurance that all is now different, but all is well.

Yogacharya David and Carla with
Christine's photo at the Ganges, 2013.

October 26

"THAT IS THE MIRACLE!"

Christine Baldigara's picture on the altar at Anandashram.

For the last seventeen years, Christine has been diagnosed with various cancer conditions. The symptoms have come and gone 5 times, with good health in between. However, the cancer has become more pervasive each time; she has defied all expectations for the length of her survival. She never cared for allopathic methods and has generally preferred alternative care and has received the most loving attention from Dr. C., Dr. L. and others.

During these past months, Christine was in the hospital and then back home and then she went into a hospice care facility. And through all of these years, George has given himself 100% in loving care to his beloved *Chris*. A constant feature has also been Christine's devotion to realizing God and to God in this form.

One thing of note, in this last year, a striking similarity between Christine and Mother Hamilton, to whom she also felt such great devotion, has occurred. Even while in the hospice care, there was something in the way she spoke, even in the way that she looked, that reminded us so much of Mother that it was a wonder. When I recently spoke to Cate, she said that during her last time there, Christine looked so much like Mother!

Before we came to India, the question came, should we go on this pilgrimage with Christine in such condition? However, in connection with this, I thought of a past trip Christine had taken to India in which she was passing through a spiritual crisis. She sat on the steps of the Ganges in the pre-dawn hours in great distress when a passing yogi started talking to her and told her about Lahiri Mahasaya's Samadhi Temple nearby.

You have to understand, yogis do not ordinarily engage people in conversation like that, and in particular, a single lady, and this Samadhi Temple he spoke of is in an ashram that is not that well known and rather hidden. If you know all the circumstances, you would see this was an extraordinary thing to happen, even on the miraculous side.

I felt that by going to this ashram by the Ganges, and other sacred places that we would be going to, all the while keeping Christine in our hearts, would be of more benefit to her than remaining nearby. So, we left for India; Carla brought a beautiful picture of Christine and has put it on the altars and sacred places of so many of India's great spiritual centers.

I had told Christine before we left that what I wanted for her was complete recovery, not just "bumping along the bottom" as her health had been for the past months; she agreed. She was "expecting a miracle." I did not have any special thought or feeling as to what the outcome would be for her, only that God should see to it that everything should be **fulfilled for the highest good of everyone concerned**. We left for India with that in mind.

As we travelled to sacred sites and met with Saints, Carla presented Christine's picture with love and light in our hearts. When at Anandamayi Ma's Samadhi Temple, we dipped the laminated picture into the sacred Ganges water there. At Master's meditation room where Divine Mother and Krishna had appeared to him, and we felt such a powerful Presence, the photo was placed under Master's lighted picture. So many places like that, to each place Christine was so much in our thoughts, with prayers for her to be completely in God's Light.

The days rolled on but no physical improvement was felt by Christine. She had hoped for a miracle of bodily health, and we wanted that for her as well. However, the day has now come when the soul has decided to vacate the body that was no longer habitable.

When Carla heard the way Christine left her body, thinking of God and chanting Aum, she said, "That is the miracle!" You see, we can think to ourselves about what we will think when we leave the body, but so many unbidden thoughts can come at that time. We can feel fear, regrets, desires, so many things can come to our minds in those last moments.

That is why Krishna prescribed thinking of Him only in life and in death (in this case, Krishna is speaking as the supreme, nameless, God of all). For the soul that has cultivated such purity as to remember God in the moment of passing, that one will ascend directly to God and have no need to return to a physical birth.

Swami Muktanandaji asked me to talk about Christine's passing during the daily afternoon reading. Whenever devotees here come to know of how she left the body, chanting Ram Nam and Aum, their eyes get large and say, "Is it so." It is the dream of all here to live in such a way to have such a death. They are so happy to know, and then they say, "Please pray for me that I can have that too." You see, it is a much valued and rare passing.

When we told Swami Muktanandaji, showing her picture to him, he said, "Yes, I remember her." He listened with deep attention to my description of her passing, then went on to tell of a great saint, Vinoba's leaving the body (I had read this description just the night before, not long before the passing of Christine).

"He was lying with his eyes closed, his face full of peace, his whole body clean and clear, the only movement being that of breathing and of the feet keeping time with the inward chant of "Rama-Hari," which in the most difficult times had never been interrupted. Just at 9:30 a.m., quietly and easily, the breathing ceased."

You see, when a great soul passes in this way, it passes down into legend here in India as a tremendous event. The signs shown by Christine during this time, looking and sounding like Mother Hamilton, her focus upon God, chanting Ram Nam and Om as her last words, these are all indications of a tremendous passage directly into God's Presence. You see how profound this is.

It is natural to feel the loss of the physical presence of this beloved soul in God. To sit down for some tea, to hear of the latest shopping adventure and what great bargains landed in her lap (usually gifts for others!), her excited description about her meeting someone in the store or at the doctor's office and finding a kindred spirit to talk to about God, or the terrible decorating scheme here and there and how it could be improved by this color or that fabric, etc. I would not be surprised when arriving in God's heaven that she should have some decorating advice for the Creator about some improvements for his many mansions!

Although we can rightfully feel the loss of our beloved friend, we can also feel happy for her, that she is now free of a body that was not operating correctly, that she had such an extraordinary passing, that the loving effect she had on so many people remains.

She said so often, in response to those praying for her and thinking about her as she was in and out of the hospital, how surprised she was that so many would be praying for her! Such was her humility.

So, both feeling the loss of her physical presence and the joy of her victory in Spirit can be felt, but in the long run, it will be the many gifts of her character and spirit that will live on in us. The best way to honor Christine is to take some of what you love and admire about her and make it a greater part of yourself: her bubbling spirit, the desire to bring greater beauty into this world, to find that special spark in another and celebrate it, to strive for truth and realization with heart, mind, and soul; whatever that aspect is, bring it into your life in your thought of her.

We pray for God's deepest blessings on those who feel sorrow and grief that the healing balm of God's sweet presence should bring peace and inner assurance that all is well in heaven and on earth. Peace, Bliss, Amen—Om.

October 27

MANDIR MOMENTS

Swami Ramdas painting in Bhajan Hall at Anandashram.

S lowly walking an oblong circuit, I join with the leading Swami, an older man who sits on a bench, and a dozen men all dressed in white singing the ancient words, Om Sri Ram Jai Ram Jai Jai Ram echoing throughout the Mandir.

I quickly become indrawn, feeling the power of the chant in me and around me. A coursing energy flows from the back of my head, through my brain and to a spot on my forehead. The Mandir loses its physical bounds and expands into Spirit Omnipresent. Now bliss is flowing within and without; what is within and what is without lose all meaning.

The rhythm of time marches forward with a feeling of flow between individual and universal, not so much as distinct, but how an ocean feeds into a bay and the bay feeds into the ocean and where they meet is both ocean and bay blended together. The thought enters, "This moment, this time, is perfect."

When I exit Papa's Mandir, the air is singing Ram Nam. The horizon above the hill sports a beautiful rising light that illumines the trees nearby in gold, framed behind with a brilliant sky blue. The scene is charming beyond words; my eyes, charged with Divine Light, make the world seem more of heaven than earth. Thus comes about this Mandir Moment.

October 27

IT IS ALL ABOUT GOD-EXPERIENCE

Yogacharya David with friends at Anandashram.

"Swamiji, Swamiji," I called to Swami Chandrananda as she walked by our door. "Is it alright for us to film Ram Nam in the Mandir tomorrow?" She smiled sweetly. "Why should you ask? Is not this ashram yours?" I said, "No, I did not want to show disrespect."

Swami Chandrananda: "You are special, isn't it?"

And why should this form be special? And yet I have been treated with such love and respect here that it is difficult to fathom. When I spoke to Swami Muktananda about departing to do the services for Christine, he said, "You can do this by Skype, would that not be the same?" I replied that in Canada they would ask, "You can talk to India by Skype, would that not be the same?" He laughed, got the logic and gave permission to leave the ashram.

Being asked to conduct satsangs, having such longing for us to come and now to return again in the future, has so touched our hearts, we feel that this ashram is our home, the inmates (Papa's word for those who live here) are our family.

And Dr. Sanheendran, Mr. Azziz, Shahina and Prakash Babu and others have come to the ashram with such love and devotion for God in this form and Nalini saying your fame is spreading far and wide. I pronam to my Gurudev for her love and blessings that have poured upon this head and ask that she bless all those who have faith and love for God in this form to be lifted into God-consciousness.

For, in truth, for this form, is only about having God-experience. He is the only goal, the only object of my life and my desire is that all should benefit and be fulfilled in having the same constant and abiding union that I have with my Beloved.

November 2

A WORLD OF UNIVERSAL LOVE AND SERVICE

Swami Chandrananda, Carla, Swami
Muktananda, with Yogacharya David.

"When are you coming again?" It was the question asked
enumerable times. What to say?

"When Papa prompts us to come." We are departing earlier than planned due to Christine leaving the body and my inner prompting that it is time to return.

It is difficult to describe the outpouring of love and kindness we received from so many at the ashram. When speaking to Swami Muktananda on the eve of our departure, I said, "Swamiji, it is remarkable, the examples we see here of those who personify the motto of the ashram, 'Universal Love and Service.'" With

Swami Chandrananda sitting nearby, I continued, "It is not only the Swamis, but the inmates as well, and more than that the paid workers, such as Omana, who cleans our rooms, and Kalavathya, who has brought our meals to us. We have found Papa and Mataji's ideal realized at Anandashram today."

As I am saying this, I unexpectedly have a loving emotion well up inside which forces me to pause, as tears stand at the edge of my eyes. What is the thought behind this emotion? It is being on the receiving end of so much love, it is seeing the ideal of Papa and Mataji expressed in so many who live here, and it also has some mysterious origins that are unnamable.

This world has gone in some wrong directions, and it suffers as a result. Too many live in a world of "me and mine" only. There are some that are driven by greed and desire nature to the exclusion of all else, and some get caught up in a world of addictions and destructive behavior that is the opposite of a life of selfless service.

Here at Anandashram, we see those who live for the realization of God and selfless service as a constant theme. Those of us who visit the ashram come for some period of sadhana in which all of our needs, and more, are provided for. But, for the inmates of the ashram, it is not an occasional time of being in service, nor do they receive all the comforts that we do with very little demand as to what to do with our time while here; rather, this is their full-time life. When there is a dedicated core number of souls in this world emulating this universal love and service, by even at a fraction of what is done by these dear souls, then this world will be changed in radical and beautiful ways.

As we prepare to leave, we are flooded with offerings of food. In addition to all the individuals dropping by with fruit, halva, and banana chips, Swamiji gives us Prasad to take back to America. I am prepared for the load, but not such a load! He gives me a backpack that is so heavy I can barely lift it! And then books from the ashram! He showers us with such grace. As we are packing our bags, we get knock after knock on the door that keeps us very busy with the loving attention of Ashramites. Time and again, "Here, just a little something I wanted to bring by." What can be done? A graceful thank you, with a look at the growing pile of loving gifts.

Swami Chandranandaji brings by gifts as well. "Since you were not able to go to Sadhana Kendra Ashram in the north as you had planned, I have brought some things they gave to me when I was last there." She presented to me a beautiful wool shawl and some material for Carla to have made up, some travel treats of nuts and raisins as well: so sweet and thoughtful.

Swamiji has also given us many sets of clothes. He has given me a few dhotis and a cloth to wear over my shoulder. When Sri Krishna saw this, he said, "You are a Shastri!" (Someone who is a master of the Shastras). By classic Indian standards, there is no way that I could be called a master of the shastras, not even a beginner of a knower of Sanskrit; the school children here who learn Vedic chanting know far more than I on this subject.

However, we have been assured by all the great spiritual masters that realizing God is not a matter of book learning or knowing a certain language. The main thing is to keep one's mind upon the Divine. Through constant God-remembrance, the mind is purified and is lifted into the divine realms. There are many who may know many scriptural passages by heart and spend long hours studying, yet they do not know God.

In this sense, you can say I know the essential nature of the scriptures, because I have lived them and I have come to know God. In knowing God, I know the Source of the Vedas, the Bible, the essence of all religions. If this sounds like vain boasting, it is not meant to be. It is simply the truth and is the truth for anyone who has come to know God through and through.

Our goodbyes are coming to a close. The car is packed with luggage. Onni, our driver, has driven to the Panchavati where Swami Muktanandaji has asked us to come. We walk the distance from our room accompanied by a dozen plus devotees keeping pace with us. When we arrive at the Panchavati, Swami Muktananda, Swami Chidananda, and another dozen or more are waiting to see us off.

What heartfelt bliss is felt as we are leaving. An earlier conversation with Leslie, who lives in India full time now, had him remembering when Swami Satchidananda, Swami Muktananda, and others were on the porch to see us off at 2:00 a.m. so that we could catch our train. With what love and tenderness, Swamiji had met us. In those early morning hours, Mansi and Lakshmi had come to our room with so much food for our train trip we could have fed many families! It was wonderful to remember that earlier time, even as new memories are being made today.

Om Sri Ram Jai Ram Jai Jai Ram we repeat again and again, pronaming out the window and then the back window as our car pulls down the drive to take us to new destinations. No matter where we go or how far we go, all we have to do is to think of Anandashram and the peace, joy, and love of God and His devotees will forever ring in our hearts with deepest gratitude. Om Sri Ram Jai Ram Jai Jai Ram! Victory to God, Victory to the Light and may universal love and service forever reign in the world as its motto and practice.

November 18

Avadhoot Saraswati

Chandra in prayer, 2005.

I am just now posting this writing and there will be some more following about our time in India. After returning from India, I have been busy with service here, as well as adjusting to the new time zone, so there has been some delay in getting these to you. In the future, I will also plan to continue to use the website for writings under the discourse category.

Morning Thoughts: Quite often in the early hours of the day, Ram will prompt me to write on some topic. These writings will be made available as discourses.[15] With many blessings, Yogacharya David.

Of Note: It was Mother Hamilton who bestowed the title of Yogacharya upon me, and it was Swami Satchidananda who called me Yogacharya David. The title Yogacharya, Mother had said, means teacher or master of Yoga (union with God). I use this name in homage to these two great spiritual luminaries in my life.

Our dear friend Chandraji dropped by, and during our conversation told us the story of the group here at the ashram who has been chanting *Hari Rama, Hari Krishna* for the last seven days. These devotees are from several villages and traveled far to be here at the ashram. They are described as simple village people who trace their practice of chanting back to a wonderful saint, Avadhoot Saraswati. I am always thrilled to come to know about a saint and a lover of God. Chandraji relates:

> "Avadhoot Saraswati," his sannyas name, as a boy had a wonderful voice and some told him he should be a professional singer, but he did not have any interest in things of the world. In his teens he left home and completed the great Char Dham Yatra (the circumambulation of India). Having traveled India, he continued on until he found his guru who initiated him into *Hari Rama, Hari Krishna*.
>
> After initiation he continued his wandering life until he came to one ashram whose head swami liked the boy very much. In fact, everyone loved him because he smiled so sweetly and was friendly to everyone. Then one day he became completely paralyzed. Everyone at the ashram so lovingly took care of him, he did not even have the power of speech.

---

15   For more information about Yogacharya David and his writings, please visit www.crossandlotus.com

Finally, one saint was consulted and he said, "Every day you must chant the Hanuman Chalisa. Even though you can't speak it, chant it in your mind." So, his fellow ashramites picked him up—it took many of them because he was over six feet tall—and took him up to a bathing tank and threw him in! Then they laid him out on the sand. He would then chant the Hanuman Chalisa in his mind 108 times. After that they would feed him lunch.

They repeated this for 40 or 45 days and one day he was able to speak! Gradually he became normal as they continued this treatment. The ashram head swami told the recovered boy that he should get others interested in chanting. So, he travelled all over India and with his beautiful voice he attracted large followings; they would chant *Hari Rama, Hari Krishna*. (It was Pabhupada who brought the chant to America and changed it to Hari Krishna Hari Rama due to his special devotion to Krishna. But since Rama was a much earlier incarnation of Vishnu, his name traditionally comes first.)

This group at Anandashram is connected with Avadhoot Saraswati. There used to be so many of them, but he is no more in the body. They are chanting for 24 hours of the day for 7 days. They divide into groups so there are at least 5 chanting at any one time. We go in and sit and listen. I was there until about 11:30 last night. Some stay there all night.

With the conclusion of Chandra's story, I am struck at how Anandashram is really a remarkable environment, where the chanting of God's Name goes on daily from early morning to late night, and sometimes 24/7. But, in addition to this devotion to Ram Nam, they invite in other groups not related to their lineage and encourage them to follow their own program.

When Nam (the name of God) is chanted with sincerity and full consciousness, a tremendous spiritual power is built. That power then goes out as a blessing to the world, so that what is done locally is felt globally. Any name of God is good: what is essential is the full faith and devotion of the chanter. Some of these names of God have been chanted for centuries, some for millennia.

May the name of God ring out now and always, purifying hearts and minds everywhere and leading all to the full realization of God. This was the mission of Avadhoot Saraswati, Swami Ramdas, Mother Hamilton and so many of the great ones.

November 27

THANKSGIVING GRATITUDE

Thanksgiving is a marvelous holiday, a day set aside for prayer and gratitude to God. It was made a national holiday in America when Abraham Lincoln signed it into law in 1863, "to commend to His tender care all those who have become widows, orphans, mourners or sufferers in the lamentable civil strife" and to "heal the wounds of the nation."

Sarah Josepha Hale, a prolific author (she wrote the nursery rhyme *Mary Had a Little Lamb),* had campaigned for 36 years to make a national day of thanksgiving before the law came into being.

However, from the earliest days of Europeans coming to the continent, a time of thanksgiving was part of tradition. When the Pilgrims arrived at Plymouth, they were ill prepared for survival. Fortunately for them, a Patuxet tribe member named Squanto taught the Pilgrims how to cultivate corn, extract maple syrup from trees, catch fish, and avoid poisonous plants. He also introduced them to the Wampanaoag tribe, an alliance that lasted more than 50 years.

Now, you must know that Squanto had been kidnapped and sold into slavery by an English sea captain and had spent years in captivity before managing to return to America. When he finally did return, he found that his entire tribe had died of an unknown disease in his absence. It was this same man who gave himself so completely to keep these Englishmen alive.

After a successful corn harvest, the Pilgrims organized a celebratory feast, inviting the Wampanaoag chief (and a surprise of 90 warriors besides!) for three days of games, eating, and thanksgiving. Fortunately, the warriors also brought a supply of venison;

the menu would have been consistent with traditional Native American fare of the day.[16]

Later, during the American Revolution, there were one or more days a year when a day of prayer and thanksgiving, or prayer and fasting, was called upon for all citizens by either General George Washington or the Continental Congress. These days were either a celebration of victories or for increasing the spiritual strength of the colonies throughout the long and difficult struggle.

Today, Thanksgiving is associated with traveling to family events, large feasts, football games, and Black Friday sales. However, we should not lose focus on the intention of being thankful and should give more than a nod of the head when saying grace before diving into a large meal, lest it be taken as a sign of ingratitude.

A natural result of a conscious connection with God is gratitude. It is reciprocal as well; a feeling of gratitude brings God closer. To make a day of thanksgiving truly meaningful, take time to remember the many blessings for which you are grateful. Even if life is rough for you right now, list those things in life for which you are truly grateful and deliver them at the feet of God; feel the connection with the Infinite grow in sacred, heartfelt joy.

When your heart softens in gratitude, you feel close to God; in feeling close to God, you feel peace, inner assurance, and bliss! This is the finest gift you can give to yourself and to others; it will truly make the day special.

---

16   Editor's Note: The Patuxet is one of 50 tribes of the Wampanoag Confederacy to which Squanto (actually Tisquantum) belonged. (https://www.smithsonianmag.com/blogs/national-museum-american-indian/2016/11/27/do-american-indians-celebrate-thanksgiving/)

Yogacharya David focuses on the positive aspects of the Plymouth Thanksgiving, leaving out the massacres of hundreds of nearby Pequot women, children, and elderly the following decade and countless atrocities that led to many Native peoples holding a Day of Mourning on this holiday.

Items on my gratitude list are for Mother, Yoganandaji, and the Masters for putting God first and sacrificing much to bring us the truth; my deepest pronams to you. And I am thankful for you, as fellow aspirants in this journey of Self-realization. We have taken incarnation together to work, strive, and thrill in the greatest adventure known to humanity, to realize God. Together we share this spiritual path; we have a common language of thanksgiving, and through our spiritual work, we add Light to this world to help bring about harmony, peace, joy, and love. Happy Thanksgiving!

Pronams,
YOGACHARYA DAVID

Yogacharya David bowing to stone image.

December 9

A FULL DAY DEDICATED TO GOD AND GURU

Travis Raney.

Travis sent this description to me, and with his permission I am posting it here. I know you will find it as inspiring and delightful as I do.

To: Yogacharya David Hickenbottom and Carla Ma.

Thank you so much for the thoughtful letter you sent us at Anandashram.

It was very blissful. Ram has prompted me to dedicate (power went out, hold on, ok, moved blinds to let in more light) a day to God in the form of the Guru, you!

That day was November 13th and started with a midnight alarm to wake up for Kriya, Ram Nam and meditation till 2:30 or so to start the day off. Ram has directed me to take no food or drink other than water and to stay in silence for the day.

Now the question arises whether one can be in silence whilst belting out Ram Nam at the top of one's lungs! But Ram says yes. The alarm again at 4:45 wakes me up and I proceed out into the ashram grounds and sit outside the Satsang Hall and count Ram Nam on a newly minted necklace of mala beads Ram has so generously provided me.

(Lights back on, thank you Ram!) About 25 minutes provides enough time to count through three cycles of Ram Nam (power out again, Ram's will!), then five minutes or so to get to the mandir for chanting Ram Nam. Since the mandir doesn't open till 6 a.m., I go to the Bhajan Hall and chant Ram Nam till 6 a.m. then over to the mandir of Papa Ramdas' to begin chanting of Ram Nam, to Ram. After each half hour of Ram Nam, I walk to Swami Satchidananda's room to quietly count mala beads (lights are back on!) for Ram and his Ram Nam Vault.

This is how Ram's day goes until 12:00 to 12:15; there is a shortened Ram Nam chanting due to lunch. Afterward, a swami I am quite fond of that is often leading Ram Nam with cymbals asks me, "How much chanting do you prefer?" Rather than giving me two options to choose from, however, he instead ends his inquiry there. My best answer would have to be that I prefer the amount of chanting that Ram directs me to do, over the amount of chanting that I want to do. However, I am in silence and indicate such. (Power out again, now I feel Ram is playing tricks on me with the lights going on and off!)

The swami then tells me that he leaves this afternoon, I pronam and bow to God in this wonderful man, then leave (15 minutes ahead of schedule due to early closing of Mandir for lunch) to count mala-beads before the start of 1:00 post-lunch Ram Nam. About one third of the way to Swami Satchidananda's room, I am prompted by Ram to write the swami a letter (lights back on) in lieu of being in silence.

The 15-minute early release provided by Ram allows me just enough time to walk to my room, write a short good-bye and return to Swami Satchidananda's room to count my routine of three cycles of mala-bead Ram Nam before the next Mandir chanting session. Upon walking to count mala-Rams I think that perhaps I should count them by the entrance and exit of the dining hall so as not to miss the departing swami. Ram tells me that I should instead go count mala-beads in Swami Satchidananda's room.

It is Ram's will whether or not this letter is delivered. Three cycles completed, I walk to the 1:00 Mandir and who do I see walking up the way? None other than the departing swami. I hand him his goodbye from Ram and continue to the Mandir without missing a step! Oh Ram, you are Great!

At 1:00 Mandir, everyone must still be eating and there is only one elderly man in the corner barely muttering Ram Nam with the cymbals. He hands them to me and bows; I bow and graciously accept my first assignment with the cymbals, Ram leading the Ram Nam, not I.

Now this man is either slightly mentally challenged or has a malfunctioning larynx because after the first verse of Ram Nam, his report back is barely audible. After the second cycle of this one-way Ram Nam, Ram decides my chanting should be continuous and gives me a beautiful melodious Ram Nam to chant continuously for Him. This continues the entire half hour, just me and Ram in this quiet man's form.

2:00 chanting has more people (Ram in disguise) but again I am there a full ten minutes before anyone shows up and the women inside the mandir motion for me to relieve them of the cymbals and begin the next half hour of Ram Nam. Ram has me sing again His melodious Ram Nam and the procession soon perfects the pitch and the chanting proceeds until the elderly swami, with the four-pointed cane, that usually leads the Ram Nam shows up and I hand him over the reins and he plays the cymbals for the remainder of the half hour. Thank you for sending me your swami, Ram, for (I am not worthy) Ram is the doer.

3:30 is satsang so the 4:00 Ram Nam is missed. Ram says that is ok. After the 6:00 ending of mandir Ram Nam, my feet are somewhat sore and the body is somewhat tired; all is for Ram though and I feel progress is being made in Ram's sadhana.

Back in Swami Satchidananda's room, there are a number of people meditating so I pull out a chair and sit in the Satsang Hall to count mala-Rams. Tonight, the hall is accommodating a large flock of mosquitos who are fiercely guarding the place. One cycle of Ram Nam is completed before I move on to find shanti [peace] elsewhere.

Returning to Ram's room (#5 of Swami Ramdas Block), I tally up my Ram Nams; up until that point 33, a good number. Swami Muktananda is celebrating a birthday sometime soon, I hear, and Ram told me to give him these Ram Nams for the vault. I am now up to 36.

That evening while winding down, I get a buzz at the door. Who could it be other than Ram? My first visitor, how exciting! I open the door and Ram is there in the form of a lovely elderly neighbor. This beautiful lady has come to bring me Prasad that I had missed receiving. Ram, how wonderfully kind you are to me, what more can I do to repay you than dedicate my entire life to bringing Your Kingdom to earth as it is in Heaven.

In the morning, I will break my fast with this mini-banana that has been blessed by You, Ram. I then fall asleep, tired from a long day of dedication to God and Guru who are one and the same. Ram kindly prompts me up at 11:30 p.m. and I perform Kriya by Ram's will to end the day.

All my love forever,
TRAVIS
AUM

December 12

CATHEDRAL OF LIGHT

Yogacharya David, 2011.

As we were ending the last hour of our six-hour meditation, I asked God, after a very full day of experiences, "Is there anything else You have for me now?"

The response I got was immediate and affected me to the core of my soul. It began with a tremendously powerful inner sound of Aum. Following on the heels of that sound, I found myself in an enormous Cathedral of Light, extending far into the distance in front of me. There were massive columns of Light on either side of the Cathedral, which only added to the light already shining from this marvelous structure.

Then with tremendous speed but with no sense of motion, I moved toward the front of the Cathedral. At the front, where the wall behind the altar would normally be, I saw a tunnel of Light. As I continued to move forward, I entered that tunnel and as I progressed through the tunnel, I saw a brilliant five-pointed star in the center; the star grew larger as I moved forward.

Without hesitation, I entered the star and then merged into it; I had left the Cathedral far behind me. My body identification was with this vast realm of Light that the star had become. My body was now the Light of the star and the Light of the star spread all over the earth and it extended out into vast, unlimited space. I remained merged in that expansive Light for some time, experiencing unparalleled freedom, peace, and expansion.

Later, when I had returned to the consciousness of this body I felt directed to write of this tremendous experience. This revelation is a wonderful meditation on the inner birth of Christ Consciousness. Through inner attunement, you may feel its truth and power, especially fitting during this season celebrating the birth of Jesus.

This Light of Christ Consciousness has redemptive power and as souls around this world join together in this Light, the world is reborn into higher consciousness and the promise given at the time of Jesus may be fulfilled, "Peace on earth, and goodwill toward all men."

December 17

THE GREATEST LOVE IN
ALL THE THREE WORLDS

Krishna and Radha, Akshardham Temple, India.

Sadhana, your practice of God-remembrance, must permeate every part of your life for the total transformation in divinizing your life. God-remembrance takes place in your deeper meditations, when you divinely love on a spring-filled day, when you are at home doing your daily chores, when you are in conversation with friends, when driving your car, when you are at work, watching a movie or in your private musings.

You may ask, "How can I possibly think of God in all those places and situations?" However, there are earthly examples when such remembrance takes place.

When you are first in love or feel a great attraction for some-one, you cannot not think of the object of your attraction. Whether you are at work, driving or at home, you think only of that one, "What is she doing now? I would like to see her, talk to her." This "love drug" eventually wears off, but when you are in its midst, it is a powerful intoxicant.

Or, when a mother has a newborn, she is always thinking of her baby, "Was that my baby who just made a noise? Is it time to feed her? Oh, look at her, is she not the most beautiful baby?" If that mother has to be separated from her baby for an hour, she is thinking, "Does she need me? Is she all right?"

If you do not have this deep feeling for God-remembrance, then you can pray to God to have it. Bhakti, loving devotion, is said to be the easiest path to God because there is nothing more powerful than loving remembrance. In that divine state of mind, it is not *work* to think of your Beloved. It is no trouble to do something in service to the One; rather, it gives you great joy! You are enthusiastic to discover what your Beloved likes. You are charmed by everything the Infinite says and does; it is the greatest love affair you will ever know.

In that mood, you will know endless bliss and joy; you are an intrepid explorer of Truth, and the relationship is, unbeliev-ably, ever-new. Unlike the human "love drug," this divine mood need not ever wear off, get old, or become stale. When in God-experience, you do not tire of it and God is always worthy of your trust and affection. God is the only attentive lover who can be with you, cradle to grave and beyond. The only limiting fac-tor in having a God-affair is what you impose upon it, for God is infinite and eternal and is always anxious to share all that He is with you.

If God is a distant thought to you, an impersonal force for you to use, an interesting puzzle to figure out, or even a close friend, you can still deepen the relationship. Whether as Divine Mother,

Heavenly Father, or your beloved Friend, any and all forms of relationships may take place with your Infinite Beloved, because God is all of that and more.

Start now, this very instant! No matter your current feeling toward God. Even if you feel distant, angry, or peevish, it is a "come as you are party!" Bring it to God, bring exactly what you are thinking and feeling. He has big shoulders and will not mind; it is only important that you bring yourself. Open the door of your heart and invite Him in, for God is the cure for all ills. Do this and know the greatest love you will ever have in all the three worlds.

December 20

SRI YUKTESWARJI: DEATH IS NO BARRIER

Swami Sri Yukteswar.**

This astonishing description of Sri Yukteswar gives insight into how great masters can walk the earth in extraordinary ways. This story comes from Paramahansa Prajnanananda in his book: *Swami Shriyukteshwar: Incarnation of Wisdom:*[17]

The youngest disciple of Swami Shriyukteshwar was Rabindranath who is now world renowned as Paramahansa Hariharandanda. They used to meet regularly at

---

17   *Swami Shriyukteshwar: Incarnation of Wisdom* (pp. 78–79).

Serampore Ashram. Shriyukteshwar requested this young man several times to take charge of Puri Ashram, but young Rabindranath did not accept this proposal as he was not mentally ready for it. In the beginning of June 1938, Rabindranath came to Puri. Before coming to Puri, he sent one of his friends to arrange for a rented house close to the ashram where he could live independently meditating and also spend time in the ashram. The friend asked the help of the ashram in this matter and a house next to the ashram was secured as a rental. Rabindranath moved to Puri and started living in that house.

On a hot summer evening, Rabindranath and his friend were relaxing on the second-floor balcony of the house enjoying the cool breeze of the sea and watching the sky. Suddenly Rabindranath thought he saw Shriyukteshwar walking from Karar Ashram premises towards the house they were in and he saw him passing them several times. At this Rabindranath cried out with great surprise and joy, "Look, look my beloved master Shriyukteshwar is coming." His friend looked in that direction and became pale as if he had seen a ghost because he knew of the mahasamadhi of Shriyukteshwar.

When he recovered from the shock, he informed Rabindranath that it was the same person whom he had met at the ashram when he was looking for the house to rent. This was an extraordinary event when Rabindranath could see his master in his physical form after his demise. After a few months getting clear indication from Shriyukteshwar to join the ashram and practice meditation there, Rabindranath joined Karar Ashram and was known as Brahmachari Rabinanarayan. Thus, the desire of Shriyukteshwar was at last fulfilled.

December 24

THE TRUE MEANING OF CHRIST

The Holy Night, painting by Carlo Maratta, 17th Century.

For this Christmas eve and Christmas day, I wanted to share with you what I read from Mother Hamilton's talk on Sunday in which she quotes from a Christmas letter of Paramhansa Yogananda. What a universal Spirit all great spiritual masters bring with them. For Yoganandaji and Swami Ramdas, both Hindu Swamis, their adoration of Jesus Christ was not just a vague acknowledgment, but it was based on direct experience with the Spirit and the man that has changed this world with his message of love for God and for his fellow man over two thousand years ago. Let that Spirit be born afresh in us this Christmas season, and always.

—YOGACHARYA DAVID

Mother Hamilton: I'd like also to read to you a Christmas letter that was written by my guru many, many years ago to all of his devotees.

Dear Friends,

Let us decorate the growing Christmas tree of civilization with the flaming flags of all brother nations. Let us drown our differences and behold the branches of our national life spreading out from the tree of one international life. Let us demand that America, India, Germany, Russia, France, China, Japan, Austria, Italy, Switzerland, Sweden, Mexico, Egypt, and all nations learn to decorate their flags on the Christmas tree of brotherhood and celebrate the coming of the United Nations of the World through their awakening in Christ. Let all brother nations contribute their best to make a League of Hearts and a League of Wisdom in preparation for their coming union. Let all nations consider themselves as children of God with different names only. May the love of nations be the twinkling lights with which to decorate the Christmas tree of world union. Let us obliterate the oddities of dogmatism and behold all religions as the branches of the one tree of truth. Let all sects celebrate around this one Christmas tree of universal religion in the coming United States of the World. Let us behold the soft twigs of our temporary joyloving senses, not projected away from, but joined to the everlasting Christmas tree of Divine joy. May we all learn to climb up the spinal tree of life and pass by the starry top into the infinite kingdom of Christ.

In this coming Christmas we shall celebrate the coming of one kingdom, one religion, one brotherhood, one human nationality, one wisdom, one evernew happiness, one language, one race, one universal law, one freedom, contact of one God, and one understanding for all human brothers. May this Christmas and New Year time fill you with the adamantine determination to improve yourself and others as Christ would wish you to do to usher in paradise on earth.

Mother Hamilton: What a tremendous vision he had of universality. It's a strange thing, isn't it, that a man from India . . . I have known two masters from India who taught me more about the Christ during the time I was with them than all the rest of the years of my life. And in the ashram where I went through the mystical crucifixion twenty-two years ago myself, there, in the most prominent place of all, was the picture of the Christ. And yet we call them heathens, yet they came to teach us the true meaning of Christianity, the true meaning of Christ, if we would only open our eyes and see that.

December 25

Happy Birthday, Mother!

Yogacharya Mother Hamilton, 1977.

These excerpts from Mother's Talks on this Christmas Day are to celebrate the day Mother took incarnation in a human body. Indeed, life would not be imaginable without her coming and living the life she did for all of us. This excerpt is from a talk Mother gave in 1978 in which she talks about Sri Anamali, a great jnani saint, sending Mother both Christmas and Birthday cards, and the tremendous lesson she taught us about free will. This also displays her humor! Happy Birthday, Mother.

Let us do some thinking before we try to order other people's lives around. Let us first order our own, clean our own houses out. Sweep our own doorsteps. And stop telling the other fellow what to do before you know how to run and regulate your own lives. It's important. It's very, very important.

I would like to see each one who is here start out this moment in God and do a thorough shampoo job on their minds, on their thoughts. Clean house! Get rid of all of the worries, of the troubles, of the resentments, the hatreds, the things that you've got against everything and against everybody and against life! Life is what you make it! You can make it wonderful and beautiful and successful or you can let it drag you down to the depths. It is up to you! You have your own free will. And you must exercise that.

I've told you many times but I'll repeat it again. I had not only a Christmas card but a birthday card from this master whom I told you about. Ten years ago this happened when he was talking to me about the complete oneness of God. There was no duality in this world as far as he was concerned. He's a jivanmukta, or a liberated soul, and he told me about his experience. He said that he was praying night and day for samadhi, samadhi, samadhi. Finally, one day as he sat before Swami Ramdas, the Kundalini force at the base of his spine started going up and it flooded his whole being. It just didn't go up the spine but it just went all the way over his whole body and exploded up here in an explosion that he said was absolutely indescribable. He said he was in samadhi and in samadhi. Then he kept praying to God, "God, take me out of samadhi! Take me out of samadhi!" (Laughter)

But, to go back to this individual will, he then made a statement (having said that there was only God) that man thought that he had free will but in fact he did not. He was the creature of whatever was predicted for him. And I disagreed with him violently. I told him that I did have free will and I exercised it. I could choose to do this or that in every event, every moment of my life. "Oh, no, no, no."

Well, we argued back and forth and neither one of us would give because we're very strong, stubborn people, both of us. Finally, I closed my eyes and I said, "God, I know I'm right. You must tell me how to convince him." So, all of a sudden, the answer came. I opened my eyes and looked at him and fluttered my eyelids a little bit, you know. "Swamiji, may I ask you a question, please?" "Oh, yes, yes," he said. I said, "You say that there's only God in this whole universe. There's no duality. Is that right?" "Yes." I asked him if God had free will. He said, "Yes, of course, He has free will." So, then I said to him, "If there is only God in this world and I am He, do I not also have free will?" He looked at me and all of his disciples sitting around the floor started snickering and grinning. Some of them were there this last time when I was just there and they remembered, and they were still grinning. (Laughter) And he said, "The only trouble with her is that she thinks too fast for me in English!" (Laughter) Well, this is true; he does have trouble with English, but, nevertheless, the principal is the same. But I love him very much and I have very great respect for him.

He has tremendous power. As I say, he's a very stubborn man but then it takes one to know one. (Laughter) So every time we meet, the sparks fly but we have developed a tremendous relationship now and we have great respect for each other and great love for each other. And that, after all, is the purpose of life: to find that which is beyond the surface and see God within each one and you will find God in their hearts, their minds, their souls. Having found that, you will find your ability to express these things and experience them expand within your own consciousness, within your own being. It's the most tremendous experience in your life.

As I've told you many times before, to realize your oneness with God inside is not to quit living but to start living, really to start living for the first time. Life is eternal; it is EverNew, EverConscious, EverExisting Bliss. And the EverNew part is the thing which keeps it interesting, which keeps it going. I don't care if you have absolute oneness with God, still you are so vast. He is so vast. And you are so vast in your oneness with Him that you keep exploring the facets of your own being forever and forever and forever because He's infinite! He's eternal! And it never stops, not until the last breath you draw in this incarnation or any other one because God is life, all of it! And life is God.

This is an excerpt from a talk Mother gave for Christmas in the year 1980. It gives you a hint of the humility of Mother, and when given a compliment, she always managed to turn it back onto God. The reference made to a "concert" was an evening event to celebrate Mother through gifts of music, song, dramas, and humor performed by devotees.

I want to wish you all a Merry Christmas, and a wonderful and happy and prosperous New Year. Keep the Christ in your hearts, in your consciousness, in every act, in every deed, in every thought that you have. Think only of him and serve him and he will come to you in all of his graciousness, his radiance, and his light and bless you forevermore.

Now, we are all invited to go downstairs and partake of the food of Christmas in the human sense.

(Devotee) Mother, we have a little presentation that we would like to make to you. You know, last night after the concert, you thanked all of us for what we'd given to you, and I couldn't help but think, and I say this for all of us, that the thanks is to you for what you are in God and for what you've attained in God, for the love that you give to us. You know, Mother loves us enough to scold us when we need it even, whatever it takes to help us realize our talents and to find God within. We thank you, Mother, from the bottom of our hearts and from the depths of our souls.

Some of you may not know that Mother's birthday is on Christmas Day, so we have two cards here. This is for a Happy Birthday . . .

(Mother reads card) "A loving birthday greeting for the dearest of all Mothers to wish you all the happiness you're always giving others, to thank you for the things you've done in such a thoughtful way, and then remind you once again how much you're loved each day. Have a wonderful birthday." There are many, many names and all this money [giggles] that I can use for God's work.

Let me say that I appreciate very much your thanks, but I give it all to God, because without Him I am nothing. He makes me live and breathe, walk, sleep, eat, everything. I could not do one thing if it were not for Him, and I serve Him in each one of you with all my heart, my mind, and my soul. And any credit for anything that I do goes to Him alone, because without Him I am nothing. He makes all things possible for each and every single one of us, as I have said. I am the littlest one on the Christmas tree of life, I feel. That I can serve God in each of you is my greatest pleasure and my greatest privilege because I, too, am serving Christ in you each moment. I'm fortunate to have my birthday on Christ's birthday.

We were so fortunate for Mother coming to us in human form and sharing with us her incredible incarnation. May you and your family be blessed on this holy day and all the days of the year. With all love and blessings.

December 27

SWAMI RAMDAS' SANNYAS DAY

Swami Ramdas, Panch
Pandav Cave, Mangalore, 1920s.

On this blessed day, Swami Ramdas's Sannyas Day, we honor the whole hearted commitment Papa made in totally throwing in his lot with God. I have included an email from our dear Swami Muktanandaji sent on the 27th and my response. I have also included some salient quotes from Papa, from his book *Swami Ramdas on Himself*.

> Blessed Atman: We are deeply grateful to both of you for the loving greetings on the occasion of Christmas and we heartily reciprocate the sentiments expressed therein.

On this joyous occasion of Christmas what wells up in our mind is the sublimity of the love of the Christ! His heart is ever shining with the luster of compassion, forgiveness and peace. It is a heart that thrills in symphony with the ailing heart of mankind. The waves of love that go out of it seek to soothe, heal, and purify the heart of every being. How blessed does indeed life become when the mind ever dwells in him.

Yes, we all remember the blissful time we all had with you during your stay in ashram. When are you planning to be here again?

By the abundant grace of Beloved Papa, Pujya Mataji, Pujya Swamiji and all Mahatmas, the activities of Anandashram are going on well as usual. They also make us aware of their guidance always in spite of our short comings so that we are constantly reminded of the ideal they placed before us.

Today is Beloved Papa's Sannyas day. He reminds us that Anandashram came into existence because of the transformation that took place in the life of Vittal Rao on the 27th December 1922. Our heart is full of gratitude to Him who not only awakened us to the higher life but also has been providing all that we need for realizing Him in spite of the fact that we are not rising up to His expectation.

Deepest love and best wishes to you and Carlaji
Ever your Self, SWAMI MUKTANANDA

Our dearest Swamiji,
How thrilling to receive your most loving note. Your words about the life and teachings of Jesus could not be more perfect, as Jesus must be seen as the embodiment of compassion, forgiveness, and peace. It lifts and purifies our hearts just to think on these virtues

made manifest in him, even as these virtues are at the core of all the great masters.

You are now a day ahead of us, so while it is still early for us, we are so glad to think of Papa's Sannyas Day even now. It is amazing to contemplate that on a human level Papa was just one man who totally dedicated his life to realizing the universal vision of God, and how that has changed the world!

May Papa's vision of God spread all over this earth to usher in a new era, an era of "Peace on earth, and goodwill toward all men!"

And, may Papa's Grace ever radiate from your hearts, minds, and souls in total realization and loving service.

Om Sri Ram Jai Ram Jai Jai Ram!
YOGACHARYA DAVID

Swami Ramdas on Himself

The great change came over Ramdas in 1922 with his life of renunciation not as a result of his own effort or initiative, but by the power, Will and grace of God. Until this transformation came to him, he was living only an ordinary life. This does not mean that he was selfish or inflicted any injury upon others or exploited others for his personal happiness. It was only that he was not aware then that there was a great Reality underlying this universal manifestation and that by attaining that Reality one could become supremely happy and peaceful, free from all anger, hate and bickering, which brought him in daily conflict with his fellow-beings.

When this great change came, Ramdas was swept off his feet, as it were. He did not know what was going to happen to him. He was asked to repeat the name of God constantly, to keep his mind serene and calm, so that it could go deeper within himself, to find the truth on which his life was based. For that purpose, he was made to give up everything, all attachment . . .

To tell you the truth, when God wanted Ramdas to leave his family—the old family you may call it—and go on a wandering life, he did not know why he was going. He went because God led him away from the place. He had no idea what was in store for him. If it was for Sadhana, why should he go elsewhere? He could have practiced it sitting at home. Still God wanted him to go. Ramdas did not ask Him why he was being taken away, but He Himself whispered to Ramdas's ear: 'Ramdas, I am taking you from place to place not because you have to renounce everything, but because you have to see that everything is My form. You have to go to householders and tell them that they need not renounce worldly life in order to realize Me.' It was with this object that He made him give up the old life . . .

Having experienced that supreme joy in this state, Ramdas was going about telling everybody that, if they lived on the lower levels of life like animals, they could never get real happiness. They must transcend all these and go deep down within themselves and realize the all-pervading eternal Spirit, which is pure bliss and peace.[18]

Our dearest Papa, we pray that same desire for God be awakened within us that inspired you, that we are led even as you were led, and that we find fulfillment in the same universal vision of pure bliss and peace in which you were constantly immersed. Om Sri Ram Jai Ram Jai Jai Ram!

---

18   *Swami Ramdas on Himself* (p. 7).

LIVING A SPIRITUALLY RICH LIFE: 2014

January 1

Standing at a Crossroads

Rama, Hanuman, and Sita, statue
at Akshardham Temple, India.

Last night, we entered into deepened meditation to bring in the New Year. Devotees travelled from Southern Oregon and Canada to be with us, and we drank deeply from the cup of bliss-filled communion with Spirit. I cannot imagine a better way to launch into a New Year, as we sent out Light to this entire world in prayer for its upliftment. I had written the words below for the occasion. Please take time to read and think deeply about the questions at the end of the writing. Life is all about learning.

We can especially use the closing of one year and the beginning of another as a time to reflect on what we have learned and apply that to the New Year. Blessings, Yogacharya David

As we close out 2013 and welcome in 2014, we stand at a crossroads. The world offers much in technology, conveniences, entertainment and distractions; from a spiritual standpoint, all of this is worthless and an obstruction.

To make true spiritual progress, the world needs to be set aside. In the pursuit of a calm equanimity, the twin stimulants of tamasic and rajasic (depressive and activating) qualities are known to be the impediments to attaining conscious union with the Divine. One must surmount the qualities of this age to go beyond the things of the body, to ascend to things of the Spirit.

Worldly nature manifests in the news with leads based on, "If it bleeds, it leads," and in advertising the watchwords are "sex sells." These are more than truisms; you can see it in action on a daily basis. When someone is looked up to as a hero today, there is a concerted effort to find some scandal to take him or her down. The world is stood on its head. If someone stands for clear values, they are seen as villains, and if someone spits in the eye of core values, they are held up as heroes. There is even less popular culture support for dharma and spiritual living today than at any previous time.

Even as in times past, individuals have risen above the environment in which they were born, so we too may strive to go beyond the values and ideals presented to us by the world. To be a pioneer is not easy as you have no support and oftentimes opposition from those around you.

To come together in singing God's Name, to support each other in living a life of purity and integrity, and to feel the joy of meeting kindred spirits is the meaning of satsang (to associate in the name of the eternal Self). The origin of the term "religion" is associated with the idea of coming together or connecting with God or with a group of lovers of God. We can draw spiritual strength when we come together for a higher purpose and feel the uplifting vibrations of such occasions. So come together often and find spiritual strength with kindred spirits. Enjoy satsang wherever you can.

We live in a time when even well-known spiritual leaders have fallen far short of the spiritual ideals they teach. When we stand for truth and the realization of the supreme Reality, we do not need to be afraid of facts, and when someone has fallen short of a lofty goal, that may be a fact, but it is also not the sum total of the individual.

When a spiritual head or adherent has acted out of desire nature or fear and he or she makes a full turnabout and gets back on track, then we can see that one in the full context of his or her journey to God. If there is no contrition on that one's part, if there is no recognition of the harm done, then that is another matter for there is no indication that anything has been learned or that the individual is once again pointed toward the Light.

Each of us stands at a crossroads of whether to go with the tendency of the world and tear down what is good, or to take the inward path toward upward evolution; it is a decision we must make daily. In recognizing that the world in general does not support the inner path, we must make a concerted effort to break the trance the world induces in individuals and en masse.

Deep and sincere practice of meditation and God-remembrance are the antidotes to worldly influence. When you feel drawn to the peace and bliss of God, you find the world loses its allure. Just as when the body is cleared of an addictive substance, then even the thought of having that substance no longer has a hold on the individual, even so the devotee feeling the active joy of God does not yearn for the pleasures of the world.

It takes time and practice to clear the body system of the attraction of the five senses and to immerse the little self into God alone. However, living in the freedom and bliss of God makes whatever little effort expended in sadhana seem insignificant in what is given in return.

Review 2013 with an eye for learning: what went right and why? And if things have gone wrong, then review what happened and why.

Let us enter into 2014 with a redoubled effort for realizing God. Double your meditation time; seek to double the amount of time you are chanting to God. And double your reliance upon God alone for your comfort, joy, peace, and guidance.

May you be blessed in your sincere practice of God-remembrance and service to Him in all forms. It is a new year, a new beginning and you stand at a crossroads that, given the right choices, can take you far in your journey to your complete realization of the Infinite.

Review: What went right and why? Oftentimes, we take for granted the things we have done well, as if there is nothing to learn from that experience. Take some time and review the things that have been positive in your year.

- What decisions did you make to create those positive outcomes?

- What can you do to build upon those positive decisions to create even better outcomes?

- Build a strong self-image according to those clear decisions and feel the strength it brings you.

What went wrong and why? Many times, we fall into self-loathing, hide away from poor decisions or drown in self-pity. Instead take some time to view your decision-making from a learning perspective—understand why you made certain decisions.

- If possible, do what you can to make restitution or to repair a bad decision.

- Trace the steps when making a poor decision, and find key moments of false logic or poor responses driven by emotions or desire nature.

- Recreate those key moments and see yourself making a wise decision; see it all the way through and experience how that feels. Then let that feeling reverberate all the way down to this moment as if that is exactly what you did. Let it change you to the molecular structure.

- Build a strong self-image for the present and the future based on making clear, positive decisions. See your God-self fully manifest and guiding you, protecting you, and ever-present in your journey to Self-realization.

Happy New Year for 2014, with blessings from God and Gurus!

January 5

Happy Birthday, Master!

Paramhansa Yogananda's portrait
at Karar Ashram, Puri, India. **

This is an excerpt from *The Flawless Mirror* by Kamala, a disciple of Master's since 1925. This writing gives a personal account of what it would have been like to be with Swami Yogananda from a unique view. Today is Master's birthday: born January 5, 1893. Happy Birthday, Master!

On August 19th (1926), we were happily busy at Mt. Washington with preparations for Swami Yogananda's arrival. The next afternoon, many students met him at the train and presented him with a beautiful bouquet of flowers. Mother and I were in the car with him as we rode back. He seemed immersed in God. Later he said to us: "Cultivate God's friendship; meditate on Him and feel Him. Be a stubborn child and knock at the door until He opens it." In the evening he visited with us for a while and said that he was very pleased that we were there.

Swami had brought fresh mangoes with him from the East Coast. The next night we had mango ice cream, which he had planned as a surprise for everyone. He touched a blossom at the table, and remarked: "In the flowers we capture the beauty of God." He had Galli-Curci (a famous opera singer and disciple of Master's) recordings and many spiritual songs from India which he played for us. He enjoyed listening to them and sharing them with us.

We attended a symphony concert with Swami and heard "Death and Transfiguration" by Strauss. We were at the Hollywood Bowl and Ralph Waldo Trine (author of In Tune with the Infinite) was there. Swami and he were acquainted. He, his wife, and son were invited to Mt. Washington for a luncheon the next day. I took pictures of them with Swami.

Those of us who were living at Mt. Washington, and other guests, were invited by Swami on a holiday excursion to Catalina Island. We were given nice rooms at the hotel and then went out to take drives around the island. We also had a picnic lunch. Afterward, several went in swimming, and a footrace followed. Five participated in the running contest. I noted that Swami's foot movements seemed to match the rapidity of pistons in a racing motor, and the long strides of the others were no match for him.

He outdistanced even the nearest one by a whole block in a two-block race! Mother and I enjoyed watching this event.

The next morning, we rode in motor boats for miles over the smooth waters, seeing many seals. Later we took a special trip in the glass-bottom boat. It was exquisite. We saw beautiful and colorful gardens under the clear water. That evening, on another trip, the flying fish were bright flashes of silver leaping out of the water, even into our boat. We found so much of interest to see and do in the happy days spent there. Swami was a wonderful host to all.

When we returned to the mainland, Swami accepted our invitation to stop at our cottage in nearby Manhattan Beach. On the way we marketed and later he cooked a meal of East Indian food that was relished by everyone. Friends of ours came to see us, and Swami delighted their two small children with some games which he taught them to play. Then afterward, we all walked to the beach, where he and one of his guests went in swimming.

Later afternoon Swami read a few stanzas to us from a book of poetry that was at the cottage; then he became very still. After a silence his eyes filled with tears of devotion. He said, "Oh, Brahma is so good to me! There is a current surging within me and through my whole body. Such bliss!" Hours later, when we meditated, I had a spiritual experience. Of this I wrote, "It is just the beginning. I can't describe the joy."

It was an unexpected happiness to have Swami come to our home, and was the beginning of a time that allowed friendship to grow and deepen with the blessing of daily association with him.

We remained at Manhattan Beach for a few days, then drove with Swami and guests to Santa Barbara. It was his first visit to our home there. On that evening, following a conversation about the plays of Shakespeare, Swami delighted us with a dramatic portrayal of Anthony's famous oration from "Julius Caesar." He gave the spontaneous reading from flawless memory. It took place by candle light since the electricity was not on then. A little later Shakespeare's strains, and all earthly drama, were forgotten as we turned heart and mind to meditation.

Afterward as we sat looking out into the star-lit sky, Swami told of the joy he felt in God. He then spoke poetically, saying the Day and the Night were talking together in friendliness, and yet each wished the other to withdraw! The Day longed to reveal the beauties of the world; the Night felt the soft mantle of darkness brought serenity to mankind.

His words became a poem, created at that moment, wherein he related a search in the cosmos for the Infinite One. He asked of star and cloud: "Tell me, in stillness, whom do you see? Is it He Who within me thrilled me with an invisible touch and quickly fled unseen?" He inquired of all Nature: "Have you seen God's hidden Presence?"

We each felt the inspiration of these days. They seemed to pass so quickly! Swami always radiated an aura of peace; one of quiet happiness. When we returned to Manhattan Beach, he gave me an autograph album. These are the thoughts inscribed:

"There is an Invisible Cord that binds the East and the West and all strangers. We are all strangers and there are no strangers since we are all of our one Father, God.

Worship Him as Bliss, the most interesting thing within you.

May He Whom I feel in the cool touch of the breeze, and watch wrestling in the ocean waves, and hear in the sea roar, and see emerging from the opening petaled-gate of flowers, be yours always in reality.

Wherever in this house I have prayed I leave an everlasting altar of devotion built in the Invisible Ether, wherein ye shall find Him always. In the self-same places quickly delve deep within yourself with reverence and steady concentration and ye shall find that secret altar."

—Swami Yogananda[19]

---

19   *The Flawless Mirror* (pp. 21–27).

January 10

Honored Guest

Paramhansa Yogananda, *The Last Smile*, 1952.**

This is a continuation of excerpts from Kamala's (a name Master gave her, meaning lotus) book, *The Flawless Mirror*. These personal memoirs give an intimate view of Paramhansa Yogananda, or, as she simply refers to him, Swami. Several of you commented on the last writing. I always love to hear from you regarding these writings. So, in continuation of honoring Master's birthday, here is more from Kamala.

It was in midsummer when there was a knock at our door and Swami, smiling, was there. He had come to California for his vacation, arriving at Manhattan Beach in July (1927). We felt blessed that he was with us. Mother and I were aware of his great spiritual stature, yet his simplicity of manner allowed our very special respect for him to blend naturally with the friendship he gave us. He brought an atmosphere of joyousness.

During his visit, Mother and I motored with him to Santa Barbara and stayed at our home there. The town had a very leisurely feeling at the time; no one ever seemed in a hurry, which gave a sense of tranquility that we liked. The days were lovely and warm. Swami swam at the beach. We went on some of the nearby scenic drives, which were very beautiful and were settings for spiritual inspiration.

One afternoon while driving, my guru went into a state of Samadhi. He was outwardly still, inwardly absorbed in God—his consciousness completely interiorized. I was aware of this and when the car arrived at the house, and Mother and chauffeur went indoors, I hesitated, not knowing if he wished anyone to remain, or to be alone. So, I stayed for a little while, very quiet, and then went inside. He came in later. I realized, some time after, that when he entered into a state of deep communion, a disciple was privileged to remain and meditate with him, and receive the blessing of being near.

He brought with him a harmonium—an Indian instrument with organ tones and a piano-like keyboard. He used it to accompany his chanting at our evening meditations.

Once we drove to Pismo Beach, many miles up the coast, and had dinner there. We always found Swami dear to be with, and his sense of humor was a kind that seemed to bubble over and everyone enjoyed things twice as much.

On our return drive to Manhattan Beach, he told me that he had seen many of his past lives and from them he had learned that the soul would accept nothing for long that was not perfection. He said: "No human being can give the joy that God can give; go to God always; give Him your life."

During these summer days friends occasionally stopped by and met Swami. In all environments he was gracious and quiet in manner. Through this quietness he imparted a warmth and sweetness felt by all.

I asked Swami what I could do in addition to the Yogoda lessons which I followed. He told me, "Meditate longer, with greater intensity, for otherwise the mind only nibbles and no realization will come." He suggested that I go on a specific type of diet for a time and I did, benefitting tremendously in health and energy. He also penciled this list: 1. Meditation; 2. Dignity; 3. Perfect Cooperation; 4. Diet; 5. Giving no cause of criticism; 6. "Make yourself better and serve to please;" 7. Seclusion is the price of spiritual greatness.

Shortly afterward Swami left with his driver for Pismo Beach to meditate. The now-thriving little sea town was then mostly rolling sand dunes. He remained there a few days. When he returned, the chauffeur said to Mother in a perplexed tone: "I don't know what he was doing, but he just sat out there among the sand dunes, facing the ocean, and stayed there every day, all day long."

Swami returned after these days in God-communion with the effulgence of that time upon him, and as he came into the room, I remained quiet, sensing his inner rapture. He spoke words to God, of me, precious and sacred; then said solemnly, "Only speak to me of God." In that vibrant bliss in which he had remained in unbroken communion, it would have been painful and restricting to turn his gaze from his absorption in the Infinite to any other topic.

One facet of his true saintliness lay in his willingness and ability to meet the noisy world of constant public life and cope with every duty and yet stay permanently in the sanctuary of inner beatitude. Here, now, he could roam in the Cosmic Vastness without even a part of his mind having to turn to the multitudinous affairs of daily life. As Jesus went to the mountain top to pray, my guru had gone by the ocean to commune with the Heavenly Father. A few days later Swami left California. He bade us goodbye and said he would keep us in his prayers. His fall itinerary included Minneapolis, St. Paul, and Philadelphia.[20]

---

20   *The Flawless Mirror* (pp. 35–39).

January 14

MASTER IS ON MY MIND

I thought you would find this an interesting description by Richard Wright, when he and Master had the darshan of the saint Kara Patri at the Kumbha Mela. Master gave a description of this meeting in the *Autobiography of a Yogi*, but of course Richard had his own observations and it is plain that both Master and Richard were very impressed with this yogi. Master had gone to the Kumbha Mela in hopes of seeing Babaji, but the great master chose not to reveal himself during his visit to the Mela. However, Master did meet with some of India's great saints in 1936, including Anandamayi Ma, Mahatma Gandhi, Swami Keshabananda, and many more. Although the focus of the writing is not specifically on Master, it does give some sense of the journey in India Richard was on with Master.

*Paramhansa Yogananda, India, at
Kumbha Mela in Allahabad, 1936.*

This is from *Visit with Kara Patri* by Richard Wright, Inner Culture, November, 1936.

I quote the following from my notes of Jan. 27, 1936: The scene is laid near Allahabad at the junction of the Ganges and Jumna Rivers, during the Kumbha Mela, the great gathering of Sadhus and Seekers, held every three and six years. We next drove down the river bed (Ganges) to the undernourished sacred river. Alighting and treading some distance through the thickening smoke and treacherous sands, we approached a cluster of tiny, very modest straw huts. Suddenly, we drew up before one of these insignificant, temporary huts with its pigmy doorless entrance, the shelter of a young, wandering Sadhu, or mendicant, noted for his exceptional intelligence and capacities, named Kara Patri. There he sat, cross-legged in a pile of straw, his only covering, and incidentally his only possession, being an ochre cloth draped over his shoulders; and this was only temporary, for soon warm days would come.

Truly a divine face smiled at us as we crawled into the hut on all fours and pronamed at the feet of this enlightened Soul, while the kerosene lantern at the entrance flickered weird, dancing shadows on the thatched walls. His face, especially his eyes and teeth, beamed and glistened with the blessing of simplicity and freedom, "doing everything with the searchlight on God."

Although I was puzzled by the Hindi, his expressions were very revealing, as he was full of enthusiasm, fire, introspection, love, happiness, divine glory, freedom, and all the other divine qualities. No one could be mistaken as to his greatness. Imagine the happy life of one unattached to a material life, free of most clothing, wearing only one cloth; free of food craving, never begging; never touching cooked food except on alternate days; no begging bowl; eats only one meal a day generally; free of all money entanglements, never handling money; never storing things away, always trusting in God; free of transportation difficulties, never riding in vehicles, but always walking on the banks of the River Ganges, or others; never remaining in one place longer than one week in order to avoid becoming attached to anything.

Such a modest Soul! Free of worldly entanglements and struggles, but unusually learned, having read all the religious Scriptures, the Vedas (very lengthy), Vedanta, and so forth, and with an MA degree in four subjects, with the title of "Shastri" (master of Sanskrit) from the Benares University.

A grand feeling pervaded throughout as we sat at this Saint's feet and listened to his noble expositions. It all seemed to be an answer to my desire to see the real, the ancient India, for he is the true representative of this land of Spiritual Kings. We bade pronam and reluctantly departed from this embodiment of God and Man, grateful for his hospitality and spirit.

And so, if I have not been too vague, you will see that there is something to this world of ours after all. Such men as I have just described come on earth to elevate those of us who are caught in the muck and mire of these passing fancies and pleasures.[21]

---

21   *Autobiography of a Yogi* (pp. 388–389) and Richard Wright's article, "A Visit with Kara Patri," can be found in the November 1936 issue of *Inner Culture Magazine.*

January 21

My Mother's Passing Announcement

Maxine Hickenbottom,
Yogacharya David's mother.

My mom's passing: I thought you would like to know that my mother left the body today at about 11 a.m., January 15, 2014.

Last night, we arrived in Sunnyside to see my mother who had broken her hip a week ago. After a successful operation, she was sent to a rehab unit where we saw her. We spent some lovely time with her, but her color was very pale, she was weak and dozed off and on. She held my hand as she slept, her life-force extremely faint. The thought came to me that she would need to choose life soon if she was to continue on. Both Carla and I spent some time seeing her filled with beautiful golden light, both of us felt a powerful vibration.

While we were there, she said that she was afraid to be alone. I told her we were there, and that she was never alone; God and Jesus were always with her.

This morning she was taken to the hospital as she was non-responsive. She had internal bleeding and needed four pints of blood; she also had sepsis due to a fast-growing-bacteria in the blood that can be common after an operation. The doctors were just starting her on blood transfusion and an anti-bacterial medication when she left the body. Thus, her life in the body ended after 85 years.

I have a mixture of love, sadness, and gratitude, and an internal confirmation that she had a smooth transition. Just this last Thanksgiving, she was wondering out loud why she was still living, a prelude to the withdrawal of life-force from her physical body.

At the hospital, Carla and I spent time with my mother's recently vacated body. As I put my hand on the top of her head, I felt heat flowing; Carla held her hand. The chant spontaneously sang through me, "My Lord, I adore Thee, lay my life before Thee, how I love Thee." Singing softly, at first the chant was stalled by emotion surging up, then my voice grew stronger, feeling her listening spirit close by. Peace and the all-powerful spiritual Presence gradually filled the room. It was a time of Grace and sure guidance into her new life. With inner vision, Carla saw my father coming to meet my mom; together, happy; a peaceful transition into a new life, a lighter and easier life.

My love and gratitude goes out to my mom, indebted to her for giving birth to this body, deeply appreciative for all the love and support she has shown me down through the years. Mothers, of course, have a special relationship with us, having known us in the womb, longer than any other person.

We have now had the celebration of life service for my mom. It was well attended and there were so many positive, loving, and sincere expressions for what she meant to so many people. Her church had wonderful decorations, and cake and ice cream for afterward. There were tears, and laughter, stories and easy conversation; all things my mom would have loved.

And as I write this, my love goes out to you my dear friend; and if you have the opportunity, do something nice for your mother, and all who are mothers, who are but expressions of the universal Divine Mother.

Pronams, and deepest blessings,
DAVID

January 21

BE HAPPY—AND ENJOY THE SWEETS

Yogacharya David's mother, Maxine
Hickenbottom, when young.

Mom had wanted me to say a few words here for her service, but to keep this time of remembering her in a positive light—and short! She certainly would not want anyone to be put to any trouble, and if anything were done at all, then there should be something sweet and delicious to be enjoyed at the end.

I always marveled at obituaries seen in the newspapers, how a life could be summed up in a paragraph or two. And yet, when it comes to capturing my mother's life, it seems difficult to do. She traveled all over this world with my father, enjoyed the Seahawks, Mariners, and Huskies. She read, enjoying mysteries and detective stories, and did crafts, like sewing all of those little sparkly things onto yearly calendars given out to family members.

She chose absurd gifts, like a cat-clock whose tail wagged and eyes swiveled in time with the seconds, a ship made of little shells purchased in some port-of-call, or the wooden drum with some skin stretched over the top and a stick to beat it with that, I am sure, seemed like a good idea at the time to buy for her son when she was in Africa.

Family was central for my mom, something that was more felt than spoken; but she spoke of it more with age and time. She loved family gatherings: food, time to see children, grandchildren and great-grandchildren. She worried over their difficulties in life and loved to see them happy. She always just wanted to see everyone be happy; that was supreme.

Her faith and church also grew with time. Her bible study group she did not like at first, "They want me to talk about what this bible verse means to me. I just wanted to study the bible," changed to, "Bible study is really interesting; it's kind of like therapy!"

In fact, learning new things was something that seemed to pick up speed as she got older. She operated her i-pad and kindle and smart phone. She was thrilled when she discovered she could receive a text I sent to her.

It really is a ridiculous notion that you could ever sum up a lifetime in words; there is more content than container. However, I did want to say a few words to acknowledge that (in how she described herself) this "simple and unassuming woman" had great significance to at least the three sons whom she bore, and to next generations of family, her many friends, and all those whose lives this gentle, heartfelt woman touched.

Now, I only hope this has been short and positive enough to suit her! And, for goodness sakes, she certainly would not want anyone to be sad or shed any tears on her account. Just be happy—and enjoy the sweets.

January 28

PASSINGS

Jesus in Gethsemane, *Agony in the Garden*,
painting by Franz Schwartz, 1898.**

The recent passing of my mother, Christine, Prem and others close to us has made grief not only something that is common to all of us, but it is also current and personal to me. My observations about my own experiences with grief, as well as what I have seen in others, has shown me there are ways that grief can bind us and place us in an unendurable hell, or pass through us in a way that makes us grow as we receive comfort from a higher Source.

Jesus said, "Blessed are they that mourn, for they shall be comforted." Now it does not appear that all those who mourn have comfort, yet that is what Matthew reported the master saying. I say this: all those who turn to God for comfort in their mourning do receive the Comforter of the Holy Spirit. Those who turn away from God either from hurt, anger or fear remain without comfort because those ones have closed the door to Grace.

This feeling of connection with God, grace, comfort, and inner assurance is what makes all the difference. When you feel connection with God you may shed tears, feel sadness, even the twist of pain in the heart in grief and yet your soul is not overcome with it. Along with pain will come comfort, peace, and even joy.

There are ways to proceed through grief that do not bind you to the ignorance of separation from God:

- When you open your heart to the great Comforter you will have a balm to heal the wound of grief.

- When you stand as an observer on the banks of the river and see/feel your grief flowing through your own heart, flowing out in front of you and letting it go, then you may experience the pain and loss that is mighty, but it is endurable and you will have peace.

- When you let go of anger, disappointment, and pain about a loss, and you do not let it separate you from your Creator, then, with time, the very same thoughts of loss that created pain in the beginning will transform into feelings of love and gratitude.

You will in all likelihood have some reaction to the death of a loved one, although it is not absolutely necessary. For instance, you may, through your connection with God, feel direct awareness of the individual soul as that one moves into his or her new life and there is no loss of connection either with the person or with God, and thus no sense of loss, no sorrow.

When that is the case, you know there is no reason to grieve for that soul, for that one is now free of his or her physical frame, known to be like a heavy, lead overcoat in comparison to the lightness of being in spirit. When in the body, one is normally limited to the five senses. Now in spirit, he or she is free and awareness is immeasurably greater, more closely attuned to divine emanations. You may experience pure joy for that soul that soars beyond this physical world, even as you might for a bird that has been long caged and is now able to fly free.

However, there may be other cases that even though you know about the current freedom of a soul, you may still feel the loss, even as you might feel loss for someone close to you who moves a great distance away. There is memory stored in the mind and body that expects that one to walk into the room, give you a call, or celebrate a holiday; with each body memory you may feel some pang of loss in the realization that one will not be walking through the door. The great Comforter will heal these poignant pains; the observer in you will see them pass through you without entrapping you.

Without knowing the eternal nature of the soul and your ability to pass feelings through, grief may very well end up entrapping you. Your inability or unwillingness to let the feelings go will trap them in your mind and body and you will endure unending torture of painful loss as they cycle through your mind and body again and again. This hell is not required, nor is it wanted by the one who has passed.

When you remain mindfully conscious of Spirit through a loss, it purifies the mind. The death of someone close to you is a stern reminder that you are a "renter" in this body, not a "buyer;" that one day death will come to claim you as well, and this clarity can lead to wisdom. When a death makes you go deeper to find comfort or answers, then you also grow spiritually. The choice of how you deal with death of the body is up to you; you may always choose the higher calling and be blessed.

When, not if, you have loss in your life, remember to be conscious in this process and let it draw you closer to Divine Consciousness, fulfilling the great truth spoken by the great Galilean master, **blessed** are they that mourn.

January 30

Mother Hamilton Experienced Consciousness of Self as an Atom

Mother Hamilton, 1961.**

This week we mark the anniversary of Mother Hamilton's Mahasamadhi, a great yogi's conscious exit from the body; this occurred on January 31st, 1991. To celebrate Mother's life, I will include some quotes from Mother that speak of her life. In the talk Mother gave below, she is having a lively conversation with Emily; the date is not recorded, probably in the early 1960s.

It appears Emily is challenging the notion that consciousness began with God and is speculating that consciousness has evolved only through creation and it ultimately became soul-conscious when it attained human birth. Mother settles the question by telling of her own experience in which she experienced the perfection of God when she was but a single atom.

It reminds me of a conversation Larry Koler told me about when an atheist was arguing his case and the other man said, "So, you say you cannot believe in God, but you believe that a rock can become Beethoven!"

Excerpts from the talk:

Emily: Does man not develop from the ultimate atom? Does he not, is he not present—I don't know how to say it—but is he not present in the beginning of the earth? We will use earth because we happen to be here. But was he not present in that ultimate atom?

Mother: Yes.

Emily: Well, how then could you say that he had ever enjoyed the bliss of the Infinite?

Mother: Because he came from the Infinite, he was one with that Infinite. And as he came from it, he was perfect in creation.

Emily: Well, he would have to go through when this earth was nothing but a boiling mass. Undoubtedly, all that would ever be was in that mass. Would you agree with that?

Mother: Well, God can create new masses, can't He?

Emily: Well, He created not only the mass but the mess here. [Laughter]

Mother: He didn't create the mess. We created the mess.

Emily: Well, if there's nothing outside of Him.

Mother: Yes, that's right. But in the state of duality, we created the mess.

Emily: It is His play,

Mother: It is His play.

Emily: He created it all.

Mother   That's right.

Emily: He created it all, in the ultimate atom, that was this swirling mass or vortex, just like our material scientists today tell us that they see this—they even call it cosmic dust, which is the vortex of another universe coming into being—man must undoubtedly be in that swirling vortex.

Mother: That's right.

Emily: Well then, he becomes the rock.

Mother: Yes. He becomes all things in gradual evolution.

Emily: So then in eons of time, in these hundreds of millions of years that this earth has been turning, we have been evolving. And you would almost say, wouldn't you, that somewhere man becomes an individual soul?

Mother: Yes, that's right. He has human consciousness.

Emily: He has the ability to think.

Mother: To clarify this for you, an experience which was given to me once, Emily, was that I was taken back to the time when I was an atom. My individual consciousness of self was in that atom. I knew that I was in that atom, and it was as though I was lying on the grass. The dew was all around me. I was conscious of being an atom in space, that I actually had consciousness, and yet I had no form other than that infinitesimal cloak of the atom. I had this experience within myself, and yet I knew that I existed, that I was perfect within myself, that I was a part of the whole.

Emily: The "I AM."

Mother: Yes. The "I AM" was there.

January 31

MOTHER'S MAHASAMADHI DAY

Mother Hamilton, 1977.

T oday we mark Mother's Mahasamadhi Day, the day she chose to consciously exit her human form. As she had already become one with God through her long and difficult Mystical Crucifixion, this did not only mean that she merged with God when she left the body; that she had done long ago. However, when she left the body, it meant we had to now seek her out through our own spiritual vision; there was no physical address for us to find her. For those of us who knew this great Soul while in the body, her death was a great loss; for those who never met her in the body, her death was a great loss.

However, she left footprints that you might follow that take you to where she truly dwells, in God-consciousness. When you follow those footprints, you are led aright, and you will know in that day of oneness that what Mother taught is the absolute truth, and that truth sets you free. Mother describes those footsteps in her talks, and here is a beautiful talk from 1961 in which the great master tells of her enormous desire to know God, and her heartbreaking compassion for this world and those who suffer in it. In the end, she assures us, none will be denied because of past errors.

Death of Ego (Crucifixion). Someone asked once, "What does it mean when it says to go to God the Absolute?" Well, the Absolute God was, is, and always will be. And He has contained within Himself everything that has ever been manifested in this world. And as you climb the spinal stairway of Self-Realization, going up each step at a time, you come to the point where you want freedom from the ego, where you want the death of the ego to take place.

And as it says in the Bible, the day will come when he who thinks he will kill you will do God a service. And it speaks of the ego within yourself, because you think of yourself always as separated from God. And this separation, this constant cry in your heart, is what makes you unhappy. This is what keeps you bound. And so the day comes when you say, "God, please take me. Reveal Thyself to me. Reveal Thyself to me. Make me see You within me. Make me know that truly God and the kingdom of heaven are within, and that there is none else in this world but Thee, none else."

And if you will persevere, if you will go through this thing called death, this crucifixion on your own cross, then truly you will have eternal light and you will be lifted up into the arms of your Father. And as you are lifted up, you go beyond all duality.

It is like a top that is spinning at such a high velocity of speed that it seems as though it isn't moving, and yet it is moving. It is moving more rapidly than anything you can possibly imagine. It seems as though it is still, and yet it has all movement within itself. Thus, it is to experience God the Absolute. It is as though there is nothing but you and God in the beginning, and then all of a sudden, you realize "I am He; blessed Spirit, I am He." And your being is filled with bliss, with ecstasy, with rapture, and you are intoxicated as you never dreamed of intoxication. Your whole being has become one of light. And truly all the streets within your kingdom are paved with gold, and the river runs with the nectar of God. And you drink forever of this bliss.

Return to Worldly Consciousness and Service. But you know that you can't stay there, that you have to come down into this worldly consciousness again and serve God because only through serving can you fulfill your destiny. Many scoff at work, and yet He who refuses the work refuses to take part in this wonderful world of God, this wonderful activity that is going forever and forever closer to Him.

It is difficult to understand this in this day because we hear so much of dissension. We see it all now. We see cruelty, and yet we must have understanding even of that. And when you have once gone through your crucifixion, when you have risen from the tomb within yourself, when you who died in sin have finally one day risen with the

Christ, then you feel the spark of life again within you. And as you look around you, you see that all of these people have done nothing more than you have done at some time or other in this life, or in some life, and your heart bleeds for them. And you want to cry because you are one with all humanity. You cannot see any difference, and you know that to the last breath of your life, you will use that breath, you will use your energy, your intelligence, to serve God and to try to take all of his children back to Him. None will be denied.

February 1

NEED NOT FEAR THE SECOND DEATH

Shushil Gupta and Mother Hamilton, the saint
Mother raised from the dead 10 years earlier.

Mother continues:

Inner House Is Divided between Ego and God. A house divided against itself cannot stand. If an earthquake was to take place and all of a sudden, this tremendous quake would just sever a house in half, that house would fall. It could not possibly stand. And so, it is with all of the things of life. It is so with the human family, with the man and his wife. You must be a united family if you are to stand on the rock of God, of Truth. It is so in your business. You cannot have a business divided against itself and have a successful business. It is so with a nation. It is so with the world. And that's why we are having so much dissension, because we are a world divided against ourselves.

Body Is the Temple Housing Little Self and God. Now, this is a great truth. What Christ meant when he said this: "A house divided against itself cannot stand," means exactly this. This is the temple of the living God. This is where we find Him—not outside of ourselves, but right in here. This is our house. And yet we are a house divided against ourselves because we have the little ego and the God Self. We are two selves, not one. And so, therefore, we must fall.

Sin Is What Maintains Separation of Self from God. And that is the meaning of the passage in the Bible where it says, "The wages of sin is death." Because sin is all of that which keeps us separated from God. It is that which takes us away from our true Self. And so, because of the fact that we are separated, then we must go through what we know humanly as death.

But when we have come to the point where we have blended this little self with the God Self within us where we can say truly, "I and my Father are One," then we have control over that last enemy, which is death.

Oneness Gives Control Even Over Death. We learn through the control of breath as taught by the masters of the East, to have complete control over our body, to go and come at will, even as Christ did. He was constantly going up into the mountain of his own being. And so it is said that "breathlessness is deathlessness," and this is so. When you can learn to do without breath and yet remain in full consciousness, when you can learn to come and go from your body at will, then you have taken death into your arms.

And then when it is time for you to throw this garment off and put on a new one, you sit in the lotus posture and you go into what is called *mahasamadhi*, or the final state of leaving the body voluntarily. You are not choked out of the body. You do not go by accident. Your breath is not taken from you. But you go of your own volition in complete peace and comfort. "He who has conquered the first death," the Bible says, "need not fear the second death." It cannot harm you.

February 15

CROWN OF THORNS

Sacred Heart of Jesus.**

When Mother Hamilton gave me the honored title of Yogacharya, she announced that I had been through nearly everything she had gone through in the way of spiritual experiences. Although I do not put myself anywhere near the same category as Mother, not anywhere near, nevertheless, I felt honored in her acknowledging the many years of my being in the Mystical Crucifixion.

I did not know at the time there were many more experiences that I was yet to go through, thankfully. I say thankfully, for if I knew the extent of those yet-to-be experiences, I may have stopped in my tracks right where I was. I can say now it was worth everything God and Guru put me through, but it is still better I did not know it all then.

One of the great experiences I have been put through, and continue to go through to this day, is the *crown of thorns*. When the Kundalini first rose up, I felt an unparalleled heat in my ajna, the point between my eyebrows; later it became a tingling, sometimes burning force at the crown of the head, behind my eyes, and at times through my whole-body system. There were other times when this Kundalini force felt like a very heavy hat sitting on my head.

It became evident to me that in the higher ages, or yugas, a king would have made this journey of the serpent force from the base of the spine to the top of the head. In later, darker ages, this self-mastery was degraded to only a symbol of a golden crown and scepter given to the king. In higher ages these symbols would have been given when the leader had attained stability in higher consciousness: the scepter representing the awakened spine and the crown the awakened God-consciousness in the highest spiritual center.

Each day I have a reminder of the crown of thorns as my head is aflame with this burning force. And each day, I hear the mighty sound of Aumen entering through the back of my head and my spine is filled with a flowing spiritual force, the top of the head is expanded, open and pointed like a spire to the heavens. There is no guess work for me to trace the movement of this Divine Force as it goes about its work within.

I write about this to you now, prompted by that same spiritual force. It is not an easy life as it goes on all the hours of the day and is very exacting in all its ways, demanding nothing less than total surrender. But I would not change it for anything, for it is as God has designed it and I am thankful to be anywhere where He is, serving God and Gurus.

The crown of thorns is really the crown of life, and when God chooses to take you through this experience, it will change you, for you will never be the same. You may be assured that it need not last for as many years as it has for me, but it will continue until its task is done, and in the end, you will be illumined!

February 26

THE BEST GIFT EVER

An old blind woman gives all her fruits to the child Krishna;
afterwards, she finds her basket mysteriously full of
valuable jewels, painting by Gargi (Lakshmi), Anandashram.

For my birthday, Jill and Carla conspired to actualize an idea I had once voiced. The idea is to do some service for others in the name of someone, then to write a story about this anonymous service done in that person's name and give the story as a gift. Well, for my birthday, I received many, many such stories; and I have to tell you it contributed to my 60th as the best birthday

I have ever celebrated. Below are some of the examples of the written stories; others were related directly through storytelling. All were touching and heartfelt and I feel so blessed to receive such wonderful gifts of love and light. May these stories spur us on to live a life of loving service to God in all forms, those closest to us as well as the one who comes as a stranger. I think you will find these "gifts" interesting in their varied and creative natures.

Thanks for the reminder. I want to make a contribution but feel a little funny writing down my good deeds—kind of like trying to get credit for something I should just do quietly! But if it makes David happy, I am all for it.

- I picked up trash along a favorite forest trail so other folks wouldn't have to look at it—thinking of David, God and Mother.

- I paid $1200 for _____'s dental surgery because she had no way to pay for it herself—three extractions. She'll pay me back when she can but seeing her out of pain is a pretty nice payment all by itself.

- I loaned _____ enough money to get home as his debit card suddenly had no balance after a canceled hotel stay. He was very grateful and it felt good to help out.

- I gave a couple at a rest stop along I-5 $20 dollars to help them out—they had a little sign and the man was playing a nice melody on the flute—*Amazing Grace*. And his flute was nothing more than some PVC pipe he had cut some holes in—the picture of simplicity. He was older and had one of those craggy, lined faces that look so worn—but it lit up into a beautiful smile when we interacted—so that it wasn't too hard to imagine him as Ram Himself in disguise!

All these little deeds can't help but bring up feelings of God, the masters, and of course David—because he does so many wonderful things for us. It's nice to do good for others with that same spirit of service and gratitude. It seems that even though we are trying to help others, we are the great beneficiaries—it's strange but doing good brings great feelings of gratitude for the one giving, so even though we may not be doing an act with the expectation of reward, we get one anyway! Hah! Isn't God delightful!

- One thing I did for others during a cold time, was gathering up about 10 coats, long underwear, jogging pants and tops and socks and delivered them to the Caring Place. These items will be distributed to the homeless.

- I still want to deliver some blankets to the outreach society.

- Brought my wedding dress over to show a young girl—she put on her princess dress and we had a party.

- Bought muffins for staff meeting and let them know it was in honor of David.

- Supported _____ while he dealt with a cancer scare.

- Helped an elderly man put his groceries into his car.

- Gave gifts of confidence to other women.

- I'm finding it hard to identify "random acts of kindness" and realize that we devotees live our lives at all times in some degree of service, and are frequently seeking feedback within ourselves as to the balance and harmony in these daily acts. As this is your birthday celebration, and since Carla sent the request, I've been focusing my "random acts" and sending them toward your beautiful, loving Self.

- In honor of your 60 years, donated $60.00 to a food bank.

- This is perfect timing. I quite often ask God to work through me, to help people . . . but on this one particular morning, I asked with much more urgency. Within a few minutes of starting work, a co-worker was trying to arrange a ride home that day for _____; she usually has her husband pick her up daily, but the two of them have had many health challenges for several months. _____ is very soft spoken and shy to ask for help. I jumped at the opportunity to drive her home that afternoon and I expressed to her that any time she needs a ride home, or to be picked up for work, to please let me know. She was very grateful; even better than that, God came through—again! This random act of kindness was a beautiful answer to my prayer, that again shows me God is always so very near and dear. I feel wonderful being of service to God in this small way, I will continue look forward to letting God use me in any way He wants. Om Sri Ram Jai Jai Ram OM!!!

- I have been thinking of this for a few days now and have just listened to a talk on how to be happy in the work place. We have had two feet of snow this past month and are giving the Antarctic a run for the coldest, windiest place on earth and my act of kindness is to not curse the weather but to thank God for the stamina to withstand, not to curse the cat, and to feed the stray cats that come to our home to weather the storm. I used to think God had a mean sense of humor sending me out to the mid-west but now I thank Him.

- I focused on Valentine's Day, channeling God's love into special messages and gifts for the random and not-so-random of His children. I felt His great delight in sneaking Valentine cards, chocolates and flowers into mailboxes, doorsteps and on desks. How much He loves His children! All as the work of His loving heart.

- We handed out beautiful red, pink, and white carnations to "strangers" on the street—I was filled with God's Joy in doing this; I could clearly see all these different faces and reactions as God Himself playing merrily in His love lila. One of the most memorable faces of God was on my sister—such joy and love were flowing out of her without restriction. I cannot remember seeing her so happy.

- It was a good experience, a contradiction to my pattern of self-involvement. So, I did a few little acts, some of which seemed to take more effort than others. Mostly what I did was to contact people who I know are struggling in some way. First, I had a few phone visits with _____, who's been challenged with unemployment for a while now. Then I had a few phone visits with _____, who sounds to be wearing down quite badly. He still has a good chatting spirit, though, and we've plans to get together soon. I also called an old friend who's not doing so well either, but is always so pleased to hear from me so that wasn't difficult. I invited her to a neighborhood party. I also sent cards with a beautiful John O'Donohue poem inserted to an old friend who lost her husband a few months ago. Last night, I wrote a kind of love letter to my sweet friend _____, whose mother recently passed away. I plan to keep this practice going because it soothes my soul as well as anything I offer.

• In honor of your Birthday, I have Sponsored _____ for one year at the Anandamayi Ma school. This is a kind act that I had intended to do earlier in the year and it had fallen between the cracks. I hope you had a beautiful day!

I have often thought what this world would look like if everyone practiced the "golden rule," to treat others as you would like to be treated. The great "secret" in giving in this way is that the giver feels such great joy in the giving that it is difficult to know who receives more, the giver or the receiver.

March 9

MAHASAMADHI ANNIVERSARY OF SRI YUKTESWARJI

Sri Yukteswar.

Today we lovingly mark the anniversary of the mahasamadhi of the great spiritual master, Sri Yukteswarji. While in India, I came across a biography entitled, *Swami Shriyukteshwar: Incarnation of Wisdom*, by Paramahansa Prajnanananda, a disciple of Harihariananada, who in turn was a disciple of Sri Yukteswarji. There are many interesting details about the master's life in this short volume. He begins the biography with the scene of his Mahasamadhi. Jai Sri Yukteswarji! Paramahansa Prajnananda states:

> It was March 9th, 1936, a Monday afternoon. In the Karar Ashram at Puri, Swami Shriyukteshwar called out to his

disciple, a young monk, "Narayan! Narayan!" Narayan, who was always present at the feet of his master, came to him. Shriyukteshwar declared, "It is time to depart from the world, Narayan! Today I will leave this body!" Hearing this Narayan was greatly disturbed and could not control his sorrow. Shriyukteshwar repeated, "Can you get me a glass of water?" Narayan quickly brought a glass of water, but as he gave it to the master, it fell down on the floor.

Shriyukteshwar remarked, "Have you noticed how I am being separated from you Narayan? But do not be upset. Your love, service and devotion to the guru are beyond comparison. I was very contented with your service. Our relationship is truly eternal."

Dusk fell and the day was about to pass. The sun was setting. Shriyukteshwar called on a person named Kruti-vasa and said, "Krutivasa! Immediately go to the Puri rail-way station and ask Prabhasa to inform Yogananda, who is now in Calcutta, that I am leaving my body this evening. He can come to Puri by the night train. It is my time to depart." (Prabhas Ghosh was a cousin brother of Parama-hansa Yogananda and an executive officer in the railway department. In those days, there were no direct tele-phone connections and messages had to be sent from sta-tion to station. As soon as Prabhas at Kharagpur received the message, he informed Paramahansa Yogananda and also made all arrangements for his journey to Puri on the same night). But Yoganandaji was not informed about the declaration of Shriyukteshwar of leaving his body.

Sitting on a small bed in lotus posture, Shriyukteshwar asked Narayan to hold his chest and back with two hands. Narayan followed the master's direction. The great mas-ter and yogi went into deep meditation. His body seemed calm and sedate. A mild vibration passed from his heart to the fontanel, producing a divine sound resembling the "Om" sound. As that sound merged into the cosmic sound, the great master left his gross body and the body became a little stiff. Not noticing this, Narayan continued his massage.

In the meantime, Krutivasa returned from the railway station. Swami Narayan asked him to sit near the master and himself went to fetch a doctor disciple by the name of Dr. Dinakar Rao, who lived next door, to examine the master. After a thorough examination, the doctor declared that the master must have left his body about half an hour earlier.

Swami Narayan stood motionless in great despair with tears rolling down his face. "Oh, Great Master," he sobbed, "Your play on this earth was remarkable. Whoever came into contact with you was fascinated by you and was transformed by your divinity and boundless eternal wisdom. Your tall body, long arms, wide forehead and strong chest, your bright, star-like eyes, always in sambhavi mudra, and your tranquil bearded face live on forever in the hearts of all who had the privilege of meeting you."

The divine child, born in Serampore on the banks of river Ganga, ended his physical existence of 81 years in Puri by the seaside. His teachings live on in the hearts of millions of spiritual seekers all around the world.[22]

---

22   *Swami Shriyukteshwar: Incarnation of Wisdom.* (Reference in *The Beginning of the End*, Foreword).

March 10

PARAMHANSA YOGANANDA'S LAST DAYS

Beloved Master Paramhansa Yogananda.**

On March 10, 1952, three days after Paramhansa Yogananda (January 5, 1893–March 7, 1952) dropped his body, Dr. Lewis, a long-time devotee of Paramhansa Yogananda gave a talk to disciples. Here, and over the next few days, we share from this talk, from the Bible, from Roy Eugene Davis and from Paramhansa Yogananda's own words. We start with the transcript of Dr. Lewis, talk.[23] [24]

Dr. Lewis:

> For the Bible reading this morning, in honor of the Master, I'm going to read the 23rd Psalm, and add a few comments.
>
> "The Lord is my shepherd, I shall not want. . . . " As we know, the shepherd is he who takes care of the sheep. "The Lord" means Christ Consciousness. And so, it is the Christ Consciousness with which the Master keeps us together. If we stay in that, we are secure. Now a great saint, as the Master, has that Christ Consciousness, as many of you know. And no matter whether he is here or not, when you're in that consciousness, you are with him. He is with you, watching over you.
>
> "He maketh me to lie down in green pastures. He leadeth me beside the still waters. . . . " Now, in "green pastures" we find luxurious growth, and it is like that illustration, if we follow the Christ Consciousness, we will be in, so to speak, green pastures. We will have all we need. Because everything comes from God, everything is in His great consciousness in all creation. Be in that. You will be in green pastures.

---

23   Yogananda's Last Days https://ocoy.org/yoganandas-last-days/

24   Editor's Note: We were unable to locate the Herbert Freed discussion Yogacharya David used in these March discourses to honor Paramhansa Yogananda. Since we know David loved and respected Dr. Lewis, we have honored Master with Dr. Lewis' devotional talk offered three days after Master dropped his body, adding the appropriate Bible references and Master's poem. As well, we added a submission from Roy Eugene Davis to complete Yogacharya David's heart-felt reflections for this Mahasamadhi remembrance.

"He leadeth me beside the still waters. . . . " The "still waters" here can be likened to the pure Holy Ghost flowing in through us, coming from the great cosmic energy, in through the medulla center, spreading out through the body, spoken of many times as the River Jordan, and by the Hindus as the Ganges. If you follow God, He will lead you in that still peace by virtue of His presence. He leads me besides the still waters.

"He restoreth my soul. He leadeth me in the paths of righteousness for His name's sake. . . . " If you unite your consciousness with the great consciousness of the Holy Spirit, the Holy Ghost, the Aum vibration that is the Name of God, the remembrance of your soul, as a child of God, will be restored without doubt.

"He restoreth my soul. . . . " Keep in that vibration. You will realize that you are not this body, but something which does not pass away. You will realize the soul.

"Yea, though I walk through the valley of the shadow of death, I will fear no evil, for Thou art with me. Thy rod and Thy staff they comfort me. . . . " Though I walk through the valley of the shadow of death: in material consciousness, there is death, nothing else. It passes away. And as we begin to rise above material consciousness and the functions of the body, the senses and the movement of the body lessen and slow down. That is the shadow of death. But, if we go beyond that, we find the great life eternal. And so, even though we walk through the valley of the shadow of death, "I will fear no evil." Why? Because beyond that is the real life. This body passes away. But that life which you contact in meditation, by deep prayer, or the Light, when you see the Light of the Infinite. That does not pass away.

"For Thou art with me. Thy rod and Thy staff they comfort me. . . . " We have the rod and the staff. Sometimes the spinal cord is spoken of as "the rod," "the rod of David." Because there is the power of the Spirit. And through the Holy Vibration you'll feel its power, and that will always be with you. That will comfort you. No matter how depressed you are. No matter how bad things seem. If you can lift your consciousness from outer things, and place it in the spine—or at the point between the eyebrows—those other things cannot exist. Because the only reality is the presence and the power of God.

"Thou preparest a table before me in the presence of mine enemies. . . . " "Thou preparest a table before me" means that in spite of all the enemies, both outward—the enemies of the physical habits, the different tendencies which are within us, pulling us down—in spite of those, the Presence of God, a table of all things we need, is there. If you will just be one with His presence, "Thou preparest a table before me in the presence. . . ." Despite all those devices of bad habits, or real enemies, God can always be contacted. No matter how great the difficulty, if you look within, (you can) feel, and be one with His Holy Vibration.

"Thou anointeth my head with oil. My cup runneth over." You know, the Sanskrit word for oil means "energy." And when you're in His Holy Vibration, in the spinal region, and rise up to this point (between the eyebrows), you feel the Presence of God, His great energy flows over you, and anoints you. These are facts. Meditate. Go within. You feel your consciousness lifted to this point, and you'll feel as a benediction His great power and cosmic energy naturally flowing through you. That's what real anointing with oil means. "Thou anointeth my head with oil. My cup runneth over. . . . " If you feel the Presence of God, you need nothing else. Your cup is full.

And finally: "Surely goodness and mercy shall follow me all the days of my life. And I will dwell in the house of the Lord forever." Contact Him. Contact the Holy Vibration. You will have eternal life. No other way. Living in outward consciousness, you will pass away, because the body passes away. Living in the eternal Presence of God, you will have eternal life.

Now, this morning I'm going to vary the service just a bit. In these difficult times, excessive speech is uncalled for. But rather I'll give you a few words, a few humble words, from the heart.

Of course, as you know, the Master has left this vehicle in which we are accustomed to see him. But, as I have said, and will point out shortly in these few words which I give you, that he is, and will be, nearer to you now that the limitations of the body have been taken away.

When your best friend, your greatest friend, is suddenly removed from you, there is a great emptiness left within the soul. And when he who has lifted you from delusion and uncertainty into the Light and Presence of God has gone, then that void seems bottomless. But, then I remember his words wherein he said, "Remember. I'll be closer to you when I leave the body, than I have been while in the body." And I feel the power to carry on and go forward, because I know that that promise will be kept. Because in all the years that I have known the Master, he has never once broken a promise.

And so I know that I can tell you: Be not distressed. We will miss him, naturally. But he will be nearer to you in a much easier way, when you struggle and try to lift your consciousness from outward things to the consciousness where he is, which is the Christ Consciousness found at this point (between the eyebrows). Contact that just a little. And the Master, as all great masters, is one with that consciousness.

We pause in Dr. Lewis' narrative to bring Psalm 23 forward for reflection.

Psalm 23

The Lord is my shepherd: I shall not want.

He maketh me to lie down in green pastures;

He leadeth me beside still waters.

He restoreth my soul:

He leadeth me in the paths of righteousness for his name's sake.

Yea, though I walk through the valley of the shadow of death,

I will fear no evil; for thou art with me; thy rod
and thy staff they conform me.

Thou preparest a table before me in the
presence of mine enemies:

Thou anointest my head with oil; my cup runneth over.

Surely goodness and mercy shall follow me all the days of my life:

And I will dwell in the house of the Lord for ever.[25]

---

25   https//www.kingjamesbibleonline.org

March 11

PARAMHANSA YOGANANDA'S LAST DAYS, CONTINUED

Paramhansa Yogananda with Luther Burbank, Santa Rosa, California, 1920s.**

D r. Lewis continues with his talk; he now comments on Master's last days:

Now I want to tell you a few things of the last days of the Master here, which I have just jotted down on the way down here. It was in the desert a few days ago before coming here, that he had wonderful experiences of ecstasy, during some of which I had been with him.

And the last few days out in the desert he didn't sleep at all, but was in that state of ecstasy. And out there he told (Miss Wright) "It may be a matter of days or hours."

And so, although we knew these many things, which I will point out shortly—as he has told me and others—although we know these things, the Lord is so clever that he keeps it from you. He keeps that which is coming from you to spare you too much of a shock. The shock is great for those who just see the final event when the Master leaves. Those who have followed and have listened carefully will see that naturally it is coming.

A few years ago when he was so much in ecstasy due to the weakness of the body from taking the karma of so many people, and he was practically gone—they'd given him up—he called me up early in the morning, and I could just hear his voice over the telephone. And he said, "Doctor," he said, "They nearly killed me today." Some nurse was really rough with the body, which was racked in pain and so forth, he said, "They nearly killed me today." He said, "I'll tell you about it sometime."

And then in a few days after that they were weeping and crying because he seemed gone. But I remembered his words, that he had said, "I will tell you about that someday." So I knew he would tell me. And so he did stay on, and he told me about it. And at that time I spoke to him, and he said, "This body, is nothing." "This shell," he says, "is nothing." "But," I said, "I know, but how about the rest of us? Why not wait awhile?" He never said. He just looked down. But he has stayed two years now—a year and a half. I'm not saying my words did it; I'm telling you facts.

And then, from then on it was a terrific fight. For a long, long time he just laid there. Because you cannot take the karma of thousands of people, thousands of people, with-out a reaction—that's the spiritual law. It is not ordinary sickness. People make that mistake. It is because he takes the sins and the karma of others. And he has told me two things which were a direct result of the taking of karma of others. One was the condition of his legs. The other was the condition of his heart.

And so, from then on, for months he laid without mov-ing. Gradually up, and walking about. He said many times, "I have no interest." He said, "It's only a few little things I have to make myself want to enjoy the senses," and so forth. "But," he said, "for a few of you, I stay." Now these are facts.

And so, in the desert before coming in, he told us, "It looks like it may be a matter of days, or it may be a mat-ter of hours." And then he came in.

And he had a meeting scheduled with the new ambas-sador from India. The other ambassador he had been unable to contact, and there was not that feeling for him. But this ambassador felt for the Master. And he was so pleased, because you know that his greatest joy was in his efforts to help India, and bring better relations between India and the United States. And he was the one who would have done it in the right way. He has worked for peace in the right way by changing the hearts of men. No actual peace will come until the hearts of men have been changed. And all of you who have met the Master know that when you left him your heart was changed. And all of you who have read his books and his words know that when you read those books, in his writings, that your heart is changed. And so, he's worked along those lines to bring peace into the world by changing the hearts of men. That is the only way to bring lasting peace. And the cause of world peace has an irreparable loss in the passing of the Master.

And now, going on—as I say, his relationship with the new ambassador from India, was the right relationship. I met his Excellency, Mr. Sen, and he had just the right spirit. That had been cemented and established in the last day or two before I met the Master. He was very happy. He says, "I feel this is the happiest day I've had, because that had been accomplished." And so they had a little luncheon at the India House, and the Ambassador was there, and the Consul General of Asia, and several others—Mr. Sen and several other members from the Indian embassy. And so we had a nice luncheon.

And that night we talked to the Master for quite a while. And Mrs. Lewis was talking to him a little bit and he told her, "It is so hard to be interested—for me to be interested in the body. It is nothing but a shell." You could see that. I'd seen it for days. But still I hoped, and hoped that he would stay even longer and longer. So he told her, he said, "The body's nothing but a shell. This is the last step." And then he said, "No matter what happens, I want you to be always happy."

Then he said, "How is the Doctor?" I wasn't there, I was in the other room. She said, "Oh, he's all right." He said, "No. He isn't. He's very much depressed." Well, Mrs. Lewis passed it off. And I will say that I had been very much depressed lately. And Monday he called to come up there, and I said, "Well, I don't feel I can go up." And I understand that Mrs. Lewis had to urge me pretty much to go, as I remember it now. Then, when I went up, I told him, I said, "I wasn't coming up, but I thought I'd like to because perhaps you'd want me." He said, "I understand." That's all he would say. "I understand how you feel." And I went up. And now Master leaves, and I see why the depression was there. The soul knows everything, even though sometimes we're not conscious of the exact cause of these things that are happening. The soul realizes those things.

And he also told Mrs. Lewis when she was alone with him, "Now, I have been cross many times. . . . " He used to give it to her. Oh, boy! And to all those near him. We got it good. I know those times. But we could never leave his side. Otherwise he would not be where he is. He said, "I want you to be always happy, no matter what happens."[26]

---

26   Yogananda's Last Days https://ocoy.org/yoganandas-last-days/
We have adapted grammar in a few places.

March 12

DR. LEWIS' PERSONAL MEMORIES: PARAMHANSA YOGANANDA'S LAST DAYS

Paramhansa Yogananda at his Hermitage
in Encinitas, California, 1940s.**

D r. Lewis continues with personal memories and recites the experiences of others:

Now I'll tell you one or two things about my own experiences with him the last few days. Lately he has been reminiscing about how we started way back in Boston, 32 years ago. He said, "Remember Electric Avenue?" That's where we used to live. "All the good times we used to have?" And I said, "Yes." And he said, "We've had a good life, haven't we?" I said, "That's right." I said, "Yes, we might have been hanging around a night club and things like that. But no. This is better. We can let go." Then he said quickly, without much emphasis, "We'll be parted for a little while and then we'll be together again." But the delusion is so great that even then I wouldn't accept it. I knew my soul went just right back when he said it. Sure, the Lord keeps it covered up pretty well.

When he said we'd be separated for a little bit but then together again, then he said right at that time, I remember so distinctly, "But remember, I'll be closer to you when I'm out of this body, than I have been in the body." So remember, there is the key. So let us not be depressed. Let us not feel bad. God is running the show. We are His children, and His Infinite Light is with us. In that Light is the Master and all great saints. There is nothing to fear except if we do not stay in that Light and Consciousness. That's all.

And so, I feel better. A load has been lifted. I didn't know what the load was, with some physical trouble going with it. But the load was that coming events cast their shadow, and the Soul knows it. And so be of good cheer. The Master is not away from us. He is with us more, and more.

Now coming to the last days when the Master came in, and we had the luncheon at India House. I stayed with Him that night and the next day, and then I had to come back here. And there was to be a banquet, as you know, at the Hotel Biltmore. And there the Master was the guest of honor with the Ambassador from India. Master had a room in the Biltmore Hotel, and he stayed in that room before going down to the banquet. But just as he was going down he told Miss Wright, "I feel I shouldn't go down." Then she said, "Why not sir? Why don't you just cancel?" He said, "No. But I must go. I feel I shouldn't go down." Then he said, "But I must, I must go through with it." And so he went down. And I know you all know the outcome and what happened at that banquet.

And so the Master's body was brought back to Mount Washington. And I went up with Saint Lynn as soon as I heard the word. I had finished my class here Friday night. And Mrs. Lewis didn't tell me until I got home. And then she told me. So we got ready and went right up. And they had brought the Master's body back and it was in his room. And he looked as if he was sleeping, as if he was at peace. And I know I'd often felt the last few days that though we hate to have those leave us, when you see them struggling just to stay to help others . . . when we know that he has said many times, "My time is up long ago," you feel, "Well, how much better that he can be always in peace." And so, that was the expression that came on his face.

And so we sat there for a long time. All sat around, of course, with much feeling, naturally. But that went on until the next day. Several were in there. I was in a room near there. And then they were chanting and meditating. A great Light came to many, and the Aum vibration was very strong and seemed to fill the room. And I know in my own case, I'd come back from sitting in the room and I was meditating and looking, and the Great Light came easily. And in that Light I could see the Master lying with his body covered with Light, in gold. Lying there just as he was.

And just right after that there was a severe electrical storm, and then things lifted and things were better. His body changed. His body remained just the same, I think, for about 24 hours, until that point, and then it began to change. You felt it began to change. The changes set in. We noticed that. And I feel that that is the reason—that great responsibility [was lifted]. Because he told me many times, "My life is different. My life is a ransom for many." If you ask, it was true.

Experiences of others:

Many others had similar experiences. I want to tell you one of the experiences my daughter had, which was very interesting. A few days ago she had a dream. She never dreams much, but she said, "It was a distinct dream; I can't get over it. The Master was there, and you and I were there, and he had us by the hand. And we were strolling on the clouds, running here and there, and I know it was in the astral." So I passed it off. I think that we were talking with Mrs. Lewis together, and my daughter said, "Well we left you out. You couldn't join us." But that was a significant thing, seeing what happened.

And so, yesterday I had called up and told her (of the Master's passing). She was quite depressed, so she came over to the hermitage and walked around the grounds, very depressed. And then she came into my apartment and sat down and we began to chant. And the whole room was filled with Light. And up in the corner came a little cross of Light. We started to close our eyes and then open them. And then she said Christ was with her—she felt free. That is the same as happened in Mt. Washington. That depression lifted.

When great saints pass, there is a great disturbance in the counterpart, in the spiritual side. And so, these things are interesting, showing that although the Master seems to be gone, he is not. He's steadfast more now than ever. He will be nearer to us than he ever has been.

As I have said, when your best friend is taken you feel, naturally, the emptiness. And when the one who has awakened your soul, then lifted you from uncertainty and delusion into Realization, into the Light, the Presence of God, when he goes, naturally, there is a great void [from the absence of] his [physical] body. And remember his words, "I am nearer to you all now" having left the body. I am closer to you than I could have been, or ever was, while in the body. So let us be of good cheer. Not be depressed, but feel his presence.

And so, in closing, let us, in this little part of the service, let us rise and repeat together one of the Master's Whispers, a part of it, a tribute to his guru. And as you repeat with me, feel that is your tribute to your guru, Paramahansa Yogananda.[27]

I hope you have enjoyed reading these descriptions of Master's Last Days as much as I have. Truly, Master has swept me into his Spirit, and it is pure bliss, even as it portrays so many human aspects as well.

27   Yogananda's Last Days https://ocoy.org/yoganandas-last-days/

March 13

PARAMHANSA YOGANANDA'S MAHASAMADHI

Paramhansa Yogananda with Madam Sen.**

In our narrative, we enter the last act, the evening of the banquet to honor the Ambassador of the "newly minted" nation of India: a fulfillment of Divine Mother's whispered promise to Master that he would live to see the day of a free India. It has been moving and uplifting to take this journey with you of Master's last days. The banquet, held at the Biltmore Hotel, was scheduled to start at 7 p.m. Master was directed to his seat at the speaker's table. Master sat between Mrs. Sharma, from Los Angeles, wife of Dr. J. N. Sharma, and Mme. Sen, the Bengali wife of Mr. Sen, the new Ambassador of India.

Just as Master rose to give his talk, Mme. Sen held her hands together in a devotion offering to Master, a pronam—a sign of devotion and respect for all Master had accomplished in bringing East and West together. The photographer, Mr. Say, from the local newspaper, captured this most significant gesture of great respect: the last picture of Paramhansa Yogananda in his living embodied form.

Master gave a short, ten-minute speech ending with words from his poem, My India. Then Master lifted his eyes, turned to the right, and sank to the floor—his embodied mission had ended. Here we share Master Paramhansa Yogananda's poem.

My India

Not where the musk of happiness blows,
Not where darkness and fears never tread;
Not in the homes of perpetual smiles,
Nor in the heaven of a land of prosperity Would I be born.

If I must put on mortal garb once more.
Dread famine may prowl and tear my flesh,
Yet would I love to be again in my Hindustan.
A million thieves of disease May try to
steal the body's fleeting health;
And clouds of fate May shower
scalding drops of searing sorrow—
Yet would I there, in India, Love to reappear!

Is this love of mine blind sentiment that sees
not the pathways of reason?
Ah, no! I love India, for there I learned first
to love God and all things beautiful.
Some teach to seize the fickle dewdrop, life,
Sliding down the lotus leaf of time;
Stubborn hopes are built Around the gilded,

brittle body-bubble.
But India taught me to love the soul of deathless beauty
in the dewdrop and the bubble—Not their fragile frames.
Her sages taught me to find my Self,
Buried beneath the ash heaps Of incarnations of ignorance.
Though many a land of power, plenty, and science
My soul, garbed sometimes as an Oriental,
Sometimes as an Occidental,
Travelled far and wide, Seeking Itself;
At last, in India, to find Itself.

Though mortal fires raze all her homes
and golden paddy fields,
Yet to sleep on her ashes and dream immortality,
O India, I will be there!
The guns of science and matter
have boomed on her shores
Yet she is unconquered.
Her soul is free evermore!
Her soldier saints are away,
To rout with realization's ray
The bandits of hate, prejudice, and patriotic selfishness;
And to burn the walls of separation dark
Between children of the One, One Father.
The Western brothers by matter's might
have conquered my land;

Blow, blow aloud, her conch shells all!
India now invades with love,
To conquer their souls.

Better than Heaven or Arcadia;
I love Thee, O my India!
And thy love I shall give; To every brother nation that lives.
God made the earth; Manmade confining countries and
their fancy-frozen boundaries.
But with newfound boundless love, I behold the
borderland of my India Expanding into the world.
Hail, mother of religions, lotus, scenic beauty, and sages!
Thy wide doors are open, Welcoming God's
true sons through all ages.
Where Ganges, woods, Himalayan caves, and men dream
God—I am hallowed; my body touched that sod.[28]

---

28   *Whispers from Eternity* (pp. 181–183), and this version https://aumamen.com/topic/
my-india-a-poem-by-paramahansa-yogananda

March 14

Paramhansa Yogananda: As I Knew Him

Paramhansa Yogananda,
The Last Smile, 1952.

An excerpt from the book, Paramhansa Yogananda by Roy Eugene Davis:[29]

On March 7, 1952, Herbert (Freed, Minister at the Phoenix Center) telephoned me late in the evening from Los Angeles to tell me that Master had just made his transition...We had observed Master's fifty-ninth birthday with him just two months before his passing. At that time he shared his hopes for our spiritual growth and publicly

---

29   *Paramhansa Yogananda: As I Knew Him* (pp. 68–70).

announced that his Bhagavad Gita commentary had been completed.

On March 4, Master hosted Ambassador Sen, Mrs. Sen, and a few others at a private dinner at SRF headquarters, and had private talks with some disciples. On March 6, he was driven to the Pacific Palisades Lake Shrine. There, he walked around the lake, had lunch with some disciples, played the organ in the chapel, and repeatedly chanted words written by the Indian poet Rabindranath Tagore: "In my house with Thine own hands, light the lamp of Thy love." He then returned to SRF headquarters.

Herbert rode in the car with Master and later told me that he had been enthusiastic about a new project. "I have an opportunity to start another work in the Midwest, very similar to this one, which will not interfere with what we are doing here," he said. He did not elaborate; he may have been referring to a project that he had already discussed with Oliver Black regarding the establishment of a retreat center in northern Michigan.

On March 7, Master stayed in his room in meditative silence until going, late that afternoon, to the Biltmore Hotel in downtown Los Angeles where a room had been reserved for him. As he prepared to depart from SRF headquarters, he commented to a few disciples, "Imagine! I have a room at the Biltmore! I'm going back to where it all started." He was referring to when he stayed there for several weeks, in 1925, when he lectured to many thousands of people in the nearby Philharmonic Auditorium.

That evening, Master was at a banquet sponsored by The Indian Association of America to honor Ambassador Sen. More than two hundred guests attended the event. When Master was introduced, before he stood up to go to the microphone, he said to Mrs. Sharma, one of the guests who was seated beside him, "Always remember that life has its beautiful roses and it also has its thorns, and we must accept both."

During his short talk, he spoke more slowly than he usually did, about his ideal of peaceful cooperation between nations of the world, and concluded his ten-minute talk at 9:30 p.m. by reciting a portion of one of his poems, "My India." As he finished the last sentence—"I am hallowed; my body touched that sod"—he raised his eyes, turned slightly to the right, and slumped to the floor. Faye Wright, and several other disciples, rushed forward to assist him, but he had gone.

Herbert told me what he had observed that evening: "When Master was speaking, now and then his eyes were pulled up to his spiritual eye and he had to use all his power of will to keep his attention focused on his talk."

Mr. Lynn was at the Encinitas Hermitage when Master made his transition in Los Angeles. When I was informed of this, I remembered what Master had said a few weeks before, at a gathering of disciples. He told us that once, during a deep meditation, he expanded beyond his body and was rejoicing in that freedom. A disciple who went into his room noticed that he was not breathing and quickly summoned Mr. Lynn, who was in the building. Mr. Lynn sat by Master, meditated, and mentally asked him to return to physical awareness, which he did. While telling us about the experience, Master said, "I wasn't going to come back. The next time I go, I'll make sure Mr. Lynn isn't nearby."

. . . To disciples who had asked Master about their attunement with him when he was no longer in the body, he said, "If you think me near, I will be near."

March 15

PARAMHANSA YOGANANDA'S LAST SPEECH

Paramhansa Yogananda holding
Autobiography of a Yogi.**

Paramhansa Yogananda: Speech Delivered at the Biltmore Hotel on March, 1952.

Your excellency, our Ambassador,

Illustrious and understanding Ambassador of free India, I bow to God in you.

I am not here in an advisory capacity. So, I will relate a few snatches of my experiences. I remember my meeting with Mahatma Gandhi. That great prophet brought a practical method for peace to the warring modern world. Gandhi, who for the first time, applied Christ principles to politics and won freedom for India, gave an example that should be followed by all nations to solve their troubles.

You, your Excellency, represent the great spiritual India. I wish that you bring the very best of my India to my America, and take the very best of my America to my India. But that is a very difficult task no doubt, for in this world nations and men are all a little bit crazy, and they don't know it—because people with the same kind of craziness mix together. But, when differently crazy people get together and compare notes, they find out their particular craziness.

Indeed, your Excellency can discover the goodness of different nations. I think if we would gather together the great men of all lands—we could build such a model civilization that all nations would eventually form a United States of the World, with God guiding them through their conscience. (Applause)

India has great things to give to you, as you Americans can very greatly help India. But we often concentrate on our faults and not on our good qualities. I remember that when I first came to America in 1920, I was warned never to go in dark alleys, lest my scalp be removed by Red Indians! And whenever I saw a bald-headed man, I thought some Indians had been at work! (Laughter)

I remember, too, that when I first came here, I was riding one day to the seashore when I noticed some "Hot Dog" signs. In imagination I saw all kinds of dogs going through the meat chopper! And I thought, "My Lord, why did You bring me to the land where people eat dogs?" I asked a man what was inside those mysterious bags and he said, "Pork and beef." I gasped in relief to find that Americans don't eat dogs. (Laughter)

One morning I was passing by an empty field next to a store. That evening as I passed that same way again, I saw a house standing in the field. I inquired of a man if the house had been there in the morning. "No," he replied, "They just put it up."

When I think of such energy, I like to be an American. But when I hear of so many American millionaires who die prematurely after making a business success, then I like to be a Hindu—to sit on the banks of the Ganges and concentrate on the factory of Mind from which spiritual skyscrapers can come and to think of the great masters of India who are her glory. Somewhere between the two great civilizations of efficient America and spiritual India lies the answer for a model world civilization.

It seems there is plenty of money for war, which brings in its wake great sufferings. We don't seem to learn from these. If we have plenty of money for wholesale killings, couldn't we picture the possibility that if all big leaders and all peoples got together, they could collect a vast fund that would banish poverty and ignorance from the face of the globe?

I do hope and pray, your Excellency, that you will always emphasize the airplanes of mercy from one country to another instead of airplanes that carry bombs to destroy. Let us work for peace on earth as never before. We want a congress of scientists, of ambassadors, of religious men who will constantly think how to make this world a better home, a spiritual home with God as our Guide. (Applause)

I am proud that I was born in India. I am so proud that we have a great Ambassador representing my spiritual India. I am proud today. I often say:

If mortal fires raze all her homes and golden paddy
fields,
Yet to sleep on her ashes and dream immortality,
O India, I will be there!
God made the earth, and man made his confining
countries
And their fancy-frozen boundaries.
Where Ganges, woods, Himalayan caves, and men
dream God—
I am hallowed; my body touched that sod.[30]

With these last words, from his poem, "My India," Paramhansaji
slid to the floor, a beatific smile on his face. He had often said: "I
do not wish to die in bed, but with my boots on, speaking of God
and India."

---

30   https://www.utkalgaurav.org/assets/img/Last%20speech.pdf

March 16

DARE TO KNOW THE TRUTH: A TRIBUTE TO PARAMHANSA YOGANANDA

Paramhansa Yogananda
playing the esraj, 1936.**

These past two weeks spent working on the description of the days leading up to the Mahasamadhi of Paramhansa Yogananda has taken me into a feeling of loving closeness with Master that is wonder-filled. His God-centered personality shines through the descriptions by various people, giving glimpses into his varied divine moods and ways that he lived his life.

One simply cannot measure a spiritual master by outward signs, although those signs may give a hint of his or her inner glory. We love to hear stories of any great saint, but to hear the story alone is a bit like looking into a room from the other side of a glass window—nice, but not the same as being in the room itself.

To enter the room where Master dwells means to enter deeply into your yogi's cave of meditation and deep communion with God. In a world of suffering and isolation, it comes as a great amazement to find that right within your own consciousness lies a treasure trove of union with the eternal, all blissful Consciousness of God. Without the clarion call of great souls who have themselves discovered this greatest of open secrets, who would guess at this truth?

This world acts as a maze of a thousand turns that keeps us from the hidden Goal. However, these same great knowers of God that tell us about the glowing kingdom within also give us the means for traversing the maze quickly and safely.

Master came to make you know that with intelligent use of your will, you can jumpstart your journey; instead of plodding steps, you may fly to your goal! A lofty promise, great words, and a moving testimony from his own life and experience that is proof of this truth.

In order to fulfill that promise, we must apply the same principles with the same vigor as the great Master did. We may doubtfully look through that glass window and say, "Well, that is alright for him, he is exceptional, but not for such a one as I." This is delusion's voice hissing to you that you cannot attain what Master accomplished. However, we must take our cue from the great Master's life, attitude, and love for God and strive as he strove, love as he loved, be willing to shake heaven and earth to uncover the hidden treasure trove!

Let us so transform our lives that we feel that we are living as kindred spirits with all the great spiritual masters. Mother felt that Master was so great that he was Christ come again. Boldly dare to claim your kinship with these greatest masters. Be inspired by

Master's life and example and know the greatest open secret in all the world.

> Part of Jesus' mission was to make visible God's healing mercy. Through his public miracles, Jesus demonstrated that even "incurable" diseases and "insoluble" problems can be surmounted, sometimes instantly, by attunement with Divine Will . . . The many instantaneous physical healings wrought by Jesus were accomplished through his knowledge of the same scientific law by which he had earlier changed water into wine: the relationship of thought, life energy, and matter.[31]
>
> —PARAMHANSA YOGANANDA

---

31   *The Second Coming of Christ* (pp. 331–2).

March 19

I AM Right Here With You

Yogacharya David, Maple Ridge, 2001.

From a recent letter: My dearest Ones,

In regards to thinking about making this purchase, I have felt that it is none other than God thinking His thoughts through this mind: having fun with His play! If we were to get to the final moment before the purchase and Ram says, "No, let it go," I would be perfectly content. If He says, "Yes, move forward," I am also equally content.

Think about how all creation is an expression of the one, infinite Consciousness, and that God is both the static Spirit that is in pure unity with its Self, and is the expressive Power that has brought all of Nature into being. In truth you and I are made in the likeness (nirguna) and image (saguna) aspects of God. We are all meant to be the one whole complete Spirit beyond creation, and the expressive power and wonder of that same Spirit in Nature.

As God creates all there is, He says, "It is good." Therefore, God (as the supreme Good) is the same whether She is the expressive Power or as the supreme Spirit beyond creation. We need only be mindful that we are Mini-Mes of God and not lose touch with who and what we really are in all circumstances.

As I wrap the shawl around me in the early morning hours, I am filled with quiet excitement at the prospect and privilege of delving into Nirguna (expressionless) Spirit. In this moment, I am totally free to be with God; I close my eyes, still my breath, and experience the ever-perfect Spirit. Oh, what privilege is mine! But not a privilege as a miser might have, for I know that all willing souls might join me in this groundswell of spiritual thrill that captures my soul, brings tears to my eyes, and puts me in touch with the all-pervasive Reality. "Oh Lord, with constant gratitude, my heart heaves the ebb and flow of the ocean of Thy love."

I was deeply indrawn yesterday and God thought through this mind, "You see, when you close your eyes the world disappears. Now, it makes no difference what room you are in, in what house or what part of the world you find yourself, because I AM right here with you: exactly the same everywhere." The Raj in a palace and a beggar living in the humblest hut are exactly the same before the Almighty Lord. So, let us close our eyes, merge our little selves into the ever-expansive and ever-new pure Spirit that our souls yearn to be.

Thinking of you now as pure and perfect in the all-embracing, ever-loving Spirit of God,

DAVID

March 22

LOVE'S WAYS ARE STRANGE!

Swami Ramdas, Anandashram.

Love's Ways are Strange!

Love's ways are strange!

It is less than the least,

Greater than the greatest.

'Tis humble—'tis proud.

It yields as the reed in the wind,

It is firm like a rock unshaken.

'Tis soft as a flower,

Hard as adamant.

It is filled with bliss,

'Tis surcharged with sorrow.

'Tis gentle and smiling as the new-born babe,

'Tis stern and grim like a volcano.

'Tis kind—it is cruel,

It wants all—it wants nothing,

It creates—it destroys,

Love's ways are strange![32]

—SWAMI RAMDAS

Papa's poem is both wonderful and terrible, for it contains the totality of life in its verses. God is the love (as described in the poem), and love is God; this is absolutely true.

You face God daily in the life that you lead. For the pragmatist, God comes in the form of practical solutions to life's vexing problems; to the mystic, life is a constant expression of Divine Life; to the depressed, life is living in a small dark cave; to the one "in love," God is walking on air. For each one lives on the same planet, but in different worlds.

You determine the world you live in by what you focus your mind upon. Think of yourself as separate, apart, and alone, and you are. Think of yourself as connected to the Infinite Being, surrender yourself to it, and you become one with God.

Love and God are exactly as Papa describes. It is the mind that determines that only when you have what you deem good do you feel happy, and when you experience what you judge to be bad do you doubt.

---

32 *Poems* (p.177).

Mother always taught, "Keep your mind on God," knowing that what you constantly fill your mind with is what you become. So, my friends, what do you wish to become?

When Krishna revealed his universal form to Arjuna, it was awe-inspiring and eventually became overwhelming; Arjuna was not yet ready to remain in the universal vision. You must surrender all that you think you understand about life at the feet of the Infinite, good and bad, high and low, and become totally open to the mind of God. It is then the mirror of your mind may be so perfectly clear that it reflects only your Divine Nature; only then may you be truly free!

April 1

SEDONA, ARIZONA

Desert sunrise at Lost Dutchman State Park, Arizona.

Sedona: God is taking us on a journey. Well, this is true in the little play even as it is in the grand Lila of life! Thanks to Rick and Judy we have flown to Arizona and have spent the last week in the *Valley of the Sun*. K, a kriyaban who has lived near Phoenix in Sun City, provided us with delightful company as well as an abundance of grapefruit, lemons, and oranges that we picked freshly from her backyard trees! We had an RV and explored the beautiful desert regions of the Southwest. In case the idea of a desert does not connote beauty to you, believe me that this desert has charming and even spectacular scenes and places of interest.

This is my first time in Arizona and I find that God is a consummate tour Guide. Traveling with Rick and Judy in their own RV, we had reservations for Saturday night at a campground near the Kartchner Caverns. The reservations had the wrong date on them and we were ushered to the "overflow" area. The overflow area was vastly superior to the other spots in the campground, sans the noise that weekend travelers often make.

"Oh Ram, how sweetly you look after our smallest comforts, making sure we are surrounded by cactus, wild hares with white cotton tails, beautiful sunsets and a quiet meditation service on Sunday morning in Your natural cathedral. How sweet are Your manifold blessings."

Inconspicuously hidden beneath the desert hills, covered by rock and sand, are the beautiful Kartchner Caverns. Undiscovered by newcomers until 1974, the caverns have been in formation for the last million years. Two intrepid cavers crawled through an opening that was 10 inches high, 2 feet wide and 20 feet long! Encouraged by the amount of wind coming out of that small opening that was ripe with bat guano smell, they continued until they eventually emerged into vast series of huge caverns with small and delicate, and immense, stalactites, stalagmites, columns and other various types of underground formations that have beautiful colors, shapes and remarkable beauty. It is thrilling to see what nature produced in isolation, what marvels there were just beneath an unremarkable surface.

We have driven north from the *Valley of the Sun* to Sedona, at an altitude of 4,500 feet. It is cooler here but the sun is shining brightly. As we entered Sedona, the red layers of columned rocks greeted us, making for breathtaking sculptures. We now have internet coverage, so I am happily able to send you these notes. W and K have once again generously given us a timeshare condominium where we will be staying a little later on.

Even while at this distance from you each day, I am drawn deeply within, and in Spirit I feel no separation at all. In the Infinite omniscience, there is no time or space; therefore, no separateness. Love flows out spontaneously—Spirit embraces all there is.

In the all-embracing Spirit, I send you all love and blessings, and may God's Spirit accompany you in all your journeys, whether close to home or far away.

Ever in God, Christ, Gurus

Reason Enough: Morning Thoughts, April 1, 2014

Gratitude overflows the heart. Oh, what gracious spiritual breezes waft through body, mind, and soul. The wealth of a yogi is in this Presence, this indescribable peace and joy. The world exists, certainly it does. With its ups and downs, pleasures and pains, yet all pales in comparison to this exquisite bliss. The larger God looms into the foreground, the more insignificant becomes the variegated nature of the world. Now the joys of the world are pleasing reminders of God's little gifts, and the pains are promptings to look to the Infinite for comfort and strength. All of these plays of opposites are but a small subset of the grand overarching Spirit. Ah, such awareness does bring gratitude into the life of the devotee; life, love, and finding joy spontaneous in the soul are reasons enough.

April 5

GOD'S CATHEDRAL

Morning near Sedona, Arizona.

Nature is God's Cathedral. Looking out upon His vistas, I sense the vast expansive Spirit that resides behind everything that is. Painting with light, God dabbles reds here, greens over there; orange and many hues of earth tones resound from every corner of this Sedona area.

It is not just the visuals of the topography, but the feeling of the purity of Nature as well. Sedona takes top honors for visually stunning views of red rock formations. Kartchner Caverns area is our favorite spot for the feeling of peace; it is where we had Sunday Service Meditation with Rick and Judy.

We drove up a switchback highway out of a canyon from Sedona and at the top was a viewpoint that was sponsored by the state of Arizona and the First Nations peoples. Many of the items for sale by the native people looked like they could have been imported from Japan. However, there was one table with a wonderful woman standing behind it who quietly said, "good morning." Carla and I walked to the vista point and returned. I told Carla I wanted to show her some clay pots I thought looked particularly nice. It just so happened, it was at the table of the sweet soul, named Elsa, who had said good morning. So, inspired by Ram, I bought a lovely clay pot with an eagle engraved upon it.

Navajo clay pot.

In Navajo tradition, the eagle is the messenger between the spirit world and this earthly one and represents strength and freedom. A piece of turquoise is good luck. The white clay of the pot comes from Elsa's Navajo home on the border of Utah and Arizona; the pot was made by her mother's youngest brother. It will serve as a lovely remembrance of this time in northern Arizona and of Elsa.

An Observation: as a guest in someplace new, in particular, one of nature's cathedrals, there is a depth of experience that can be had for the sensitive soul. To get this depth, you must have a certain attunement to the subtle world that resides just behind this gross material one.

I have observed that the majority of people who tour a new place are engaged in conversation with others about times and places other than where they are at. Such a preoccupation excludes the more subtle plane of inner experience. To feel the soul of a place, or the lack of it, to be aware of the spirit that may be present, one must be focused in the present and open to this inner awareness.

Today we walked the trails of Walnut Canyon, near Flagstaff, and it was just such a place where there was much more than what met the eye. The attraction of the canyon is the cave-like structures that were used for a generation or two by the native Hopi Nation. However, the place is ripe with spiritual meaning for the local tribes as they have used this area as a site for sacred ceremonies stretching back into time untold.

Climbing down the paths of the steep-sided canyon, the rustic dwellings spoke of a time of great need. A volcanic eruption (in what was later to become Flagstaff Arizona) sent the local inhabitants off to alternative locations for homes, fields for growing food, and areas to hunt game. Thus, the sacred site was used for this purpose; over time it proved unsuitable to sustain the livelihood of the tribal members; they moved on. However, the hundreds and hundreds of years of using this site for sacred ceremonies and finding healing herbs makes for a tremendous radiation of peaceful vibration that is distinct and palpable.

At 6,000 feet above sea level, Walnut Canyon sits at a similar altitude as Babaji's Cave, and with pine trees, cactus, and a variety of healing herbs, it has a familiar feel to it from our pilgrimages to Dronagiri. For Carla and I, the area spoke of a natural and human-created place of peace.

It is a lesson for all in our journeys in life, for God is all and all in all. To become too commonplace in our thoughts is to miss the deeper meaning of our journey, an opportunity never to be captured again.

April 11

MY NEW FAVORITE PLACE

Tonto Natural Bridge.

"This is my new favorite place!" Carla said this as we were at the base of Tonto Natural Bridge. The land bridge is the world's largest travertine (400 feet long, 183 feet high, 150 feet wide), a formation that is created by a hot spring pouring over the sides, leaving a buildup of minerals over millennia.

The land bridge was first known by settlers when a miner was chased by Apaches and he hid in one of the caves nearby. Today it is a state park that requires a steep drive down and then a switch-back trail that takes you to the base of the bridge.

It is when we arrive at the end of the trail that we are charmed by the red rock slabs surrounding pools of water under this natural bridge. There are many caves that captivate our interest. It always intrigues me to be inside these caves.

Carla near Tonto Natural Bridge.

From time immemorial, caves have been the natural habitat of yogis, monks, and spiritual seekers. There are practical reasons for this: a cave will provide shelter, and with a little fire, a cave can become a comfortable living site.

There are also more subtle reasons for an inwardly-focused meditator to find a cave suitable. As you spiritually progress, your psychic body becomes more sensitive, more open. Noise, light and mental disturbances by worldly people can become difficult, even painful for the ardent seeker. The refuge of the cave blocks out sound and light and is an excellent insulator from the psychic chaos of the world.

There are places upon the earth that are naturally attuned to more refined spiritual forces. An area or a cave can also become spiritually charged due to the influence of a highly advanced soul. The two can work together when a naturally charged area is frequented by a highly developed being, an ultimate combination of nature and nurture.

Under the land bridge, there are a number of naturally formed caves. There is no evidence of any advanced soul having lived here, but there is a profound sense of peace and spiritual vibrancy that accompanies this natural setting. In our journey to the Southwest, we had previously felt such a vibration at Kartchner Caverns State Park. Now, here, it is felt to be even more powerful.

God arranged it so that just as we arrive, a group of hikers is leaving, giving the place all to ourselves. We explore around the pools of water and sit in the natural caves. It is a spiritual baptism for the soul, washing clean everything not of a higher vibration.

Yogacharya David in cave near Tonto Natural Bridge.

It is inevitable that when we mix with the world, we will pick up some of those lower influences. The advanced practitioner may rise above these influences. Some may be divinely directed to purify such forces through their bodies and the most advanced in consciousness will simply see these forces as aspects of God.

When Papa Ramdas had a vision of Krishna, he said something to Krishna that was shocking to me when I first read it. Papa told Krishna to take this form of Krishna away and to make Papa see

Krishna in His universal form, the all-pervading universal vision. There are many aspirants who seek all of their lives for the embodiment of Krishna to manifest even as he did to Papa, yet here was Papa sending him away! Papa was after the purist, most sublime vision of God, not a form that can come and go, but a permanent vision of God as everything that is!

Water pool near Tonto Natural Bridge.

As I have said before, God is equally present everywhere, it is just that he seems more *equally Present* in some places than others! The spontaneous thought comes to me now, that you should feel the peace and spiritual purity of this sanctuary of God under that natural land bridge and that as we imbibe the deep Presence of the Divine in God's natural cathedrals, you will be with us in Spirit and feel it as well.

May 11

HAPPY MOTHER'S DAY

Rose blossom.

I want to wish all mothers a special blessing of love and gratitude. Without mothers this human race would vanish! By going into the jaws of death to bring forth new life, a mother only begins her journey of motherhood. And there is an even greater role for all mothers, for all women—each one is a manifestation of the Divine Mother. So, to all women, I bow at your feet in love and gratitude for your unique contributions as expressions of beloved Divine Mother.

I thought I would send this excerpt of a talk from Mother that is sure to put a smile on your face:

Mother's Day

by The Reverend Mother,
Yogacharya M. Hamilton
May 13, 1979

I want to thank all of you for your prayers for me. As you know, I didn't have my surgery. But I think it was your prayers that kept me from having it because, obviously, I was in no condition to have it. And if it hadn't been for the prayers, I might not have known that. The surgery is scheduled for next Friday, so I'll appreciate your continuing them.

I want to read to you this morning, because it's Mother's Day, "A Mother's Prayer."

Dear Lord, please help me understand my four boys, not including my husband.

Dear Lord, that means five adolescents, including my husband.

Dear Lord, please help me teach my sons how to stand on their own two feet and at the same time not step on somebody else's toes. And help me appease four different kinds of appetite at each meal. And help me find a ready cure for acne so that everybody in the house can eat chocolate cake the same year. And help me serve a main course at dinner my sons have not had at school for lunch that day. And help my husband give them a smack when it's called for instead of an increase in allowance.

Dear Lord, please help me not to hear so much, see so much and say so much. And help me not to correct so much. And help somebody invent a hi-fi that will play so loud and no louder. And help my boys talk about something besides baseball because I can't have Tallulah Bankhead for dinner with them every night. And help find a way for them to learn their piano lesson in only ten minutes of practice a day. And help me once in a while have my hair cut instead of pulling it. And help hand-me-downs fit somebody after being in the closet three years.

Dear Lord, please help me to explain to Jeff that he does not have to approve of the girls Warren and George take out. And help me remember to buy name tapes. And help me have the patience to sew them on. And help me talk softly and carry a big layer cake. And help me find a dessert that is not bad for weight, skin and teeth and that all my sons will like the same night. And help me find a dress that all my five men and I will like.

Dear Lord, please make geometry go away. And please help me understand space, even if there is none in my closets. And help my boys find girls someday who are good enough for them even though I won't think so at the time. And help Fordham Law School teach George as much about Blackstone as he now knows about Spinks Baseball Guide. And help Columbia University teach Warren there is something else in the world besides the theater and music. And help Jeffrey believe that giving up catsup, at least for breakfast, will improve his chances for becoming a bullfighter. And help Douglas at twelve feel like sixteen. Me, too.

Dear Lord, please accept my thanks for giving my boys a sense of humor, if it is often at my expense— which is too expensive. And thank you for George's liking Wallstreet quotations and not the drums. And thank you for Warren's liking the piano and not the drums. And thank you for Jeffrey's liking the guitar and not the drums. And thank you for Douglas' liking science and not the drums.

Dear Lord, thank you, thank you, thank you for my husband and for giving us four sons. Dear Lord.

(Laughter) I had to share that with you. It's beautiful.

May 23

Memorial Day

Since childhood, Memorial Day has been a special family celebration. Although the holiday was launched to pay respects to those who gave their lives in war, for many it was expanded to give honor and to remember all of our ancestors.

Each year it has been our family's tradition to take flowers out to all the gravesites in the area that was first settled in the mid-to-late 1800s. My great grandfather moved onto undeveloped land covered only by rock and sagebrush, built his tent, and walked five miles round trip to the river, with a yoke and buckets, to get water for drinking, watering his fruit trees, and washing. He knew the irrigation canal would arrive in a couple of years, so he endured; bringing his new wife to his tent home in January, a cold and dismal time of the year. He and many of his progeny are buried in an ancient cemetery that overlooks that same Yakima River he had walked to every day in those early years.

Now, at a time when there is so much looking forward to what is coming in a rapidly changing world, it is good to take time to look back, and honor those who gave so much for their families and for securing a better future. In relative terms, we live in such prosperous times, thanks to those core principles that were in the hearts and minds of so many of the past, and it would be good to emulate many of those now.

"A man is as good as his word," was taken very seriously where I grew up. Far more importantly than a person's social status or ethnicity was his integrity. That you were slow to borrow money, and you paid it back as soon as you could was highly valued; and you did not leave a debt unpaid. You worked hard, often from early sun to late in the day, and during harvest time you may go as long as light was available, for crops ready to harvest would not wait. Prayer was done quietly, but seriously. The town I grew up in was once in the Guinness World Records as having the most churches per population.

These are some of the lessons that were all around me when growing up. I honor those who have gone before, worked hard, were honest in their dealings with their fellow man and in general strove to live good lives. Of course, there were plenty of heartbreaks along the way, those who did not live according to those high principles, and plenty of "characters" who added color and liveliness to the landscape.

As in any family, there is plenty of pain that has been handed down. We have all been recipients of a pretty rough couple of thousand years in which man's inhumanity to man has been atrocious. Wars, famines, and cruelty, both institutionally and personally, left little room for many to be even aware that there might be a better, higher way to Self-realization. However, there have always been those who have risen above their times.

And this leads to another area in which to honor ancestors of a different type. Spiritually-kindred spirits will many times be as important, and even more so, than blood relationships in our lives. I would not have had physical incarnation was it not for my human mother and father, and I would not have had my spiritual birth if not for Mother Hamilton and our succession of para-param gurus. The second could not be without the first birth, but the second, the spiritual birth, is the more important.

I lay the flowers of devotion upon the "markers" of the guru's spiritually-enlightened lives. Those markers are the spiritual Light they brought into this world; for this I am so truly grateful. I bow at their feet in love and adoration, now and for all time. And to you, my spiritual family, I join with you in the celebration of the great gift given to us by these luminary giants that make us kindred spirits with the deepest bonds of love and the profound desire to rise up to the Light of lights where all sorrow is resolved in bliss and understanding. Ever in God Christ Gurus.

Mother Hamilton with Yogacharya
David, drawing by Lorraine Bourcier.

September 20

FIRE AND GRACE

My Dear Friends,
It was Memorial Day since my last posting. I am now resuming the posts after this summer hiatus.

The intensity of my inner and outer experiences over the summer has been quite something. The Baptism of Fire hinted at by Jesus is an internal conflagration of vast proportions. For some entering the Mystical Crucifixion, this baptism of fire is of relatively short duration. But in certain cases, Divine Will uses this fire to help purify not only His devotee, but for the greater good as well. Therefore, this fire may extend over many years, or even the span of a life, in rare cases.

This fire may or may not create heat in the physical body, but it definitely rages through the subtle body. I have lived with this Baptism of Fire for nearly forty years now. In the beginning, the purpose was more to do with this body and the karma associated with it. Then it gradually began to be of help to others, and in this third stage it has to do with being of service to this world. So, the notion of suffering in *eternal fire* has a certain ring of familiarity to it for me!

It has not been all fire; there is also the settling into the new house. Coinciding with moving in was having Kriya Initiation in our lovely Meditation Hall on the lower floor. Even days before the Initiation Classes were to start, a powerful charge began to build in the house; the masters were gathering. What wonderful souls gathered, each one beginning a new life of spiritual exploration.

We are continuing to settle in, organizing storage mostly. Every day brings new adventure in the Divine. A realization that comes again and again is how vast this search really is. There are some areas where seeing how much there is to know can be disheartening, but not with God. With spiritual realization, there is only awe and inspiration to know that when we reach for the infinite, there is a promise of more Light, more bliss, and more revelations of deeper Truth! It is inspiring beyond all words.

And with that Journey of journeys wide open before us, with simply the will to explore needed to do so, I stand with you, hand-in-hand, to begin ever-new the great adventure in God.

Yogacharya David at Kriya Initiation, 2011.**

September 22

FALL EQUINOX

Paramhansa Yogananda and Sri Yukteswar, Serampore, 1935.

The Fall Equinox is on September 22, at about 7:30 p.m. The equinox (equal night) is when the days and nights are of the same length and we are halfway between summer (longest day) and winter solstice (the shortest day). The two equinoxes and two solstices are four transitions in the year that have been marked by civilizations since recorded time.

Besides the fall equinox being a time of harvest and thanksgiving, it is also known to be a special opportunity for focusing on things spiritual. Spring, summer, fall, and winter each have their beginning and end, and each of these yearly cycles corresponds to times in the day, early morning, noon, evening, and midnight. Sensitive yogis noticed that these times of the day and times of the year present an opening into higher consciousness for the meditator.

Therefore, Sri Yukteswar kept these times for coming together in song, food, and a particular focus on spiritual upliftment. In *The Autobiography of a Yogi*, Master writes:[33]

> Sri Yukteswar sponsored four yearly festivals, at the equi-noxes and solstices, when his students gathered from far and near. The winter solstice celebration was held in Serampore; the first one I attended left me with a perma-nent blessing.
>
> The festivities started in the morning with a barefoot procession along the streets. The voices of a hundred stu-dents rang out with sweet religious songs; a few musi-cians played the flute and *khol kartal* (drums and cymbals). Enthusiastic townspeople strewed the path with flowers, glad to be summoned from prosaic tasks by our resound-ing praise of the Lord's blessed name. The long tour ended in the courtyard of the hermitage. There we encir-cled our guru, while students on upper balconies show-ered us with marigold blossoms.
>
> Many guests went upstairs to receive a pudding of *channa* and oranges. I made my way to a group of brother disciples who were serving today as cooks. Food for such large gatherings had to be cooked outdoors in huge caul-drons. The improvised wood-burning brick stoves were smoky and tear-provoking, but we laughed merrily at our work. Religious festivals in India are never considered troublesome; each one does his part, supplying money, rice, vegetables, or his personal services.

---

33   *Autobiography of a Yogi* (p. 156).

. . . By sunset we had served our hundreds of visitors with *khichuri* (rice and lentils), vegetable curry, and rice pudding. We laid cotton blankets over the courtyard; soon the assemblage was squatting under the starry vault, quietly attentive to the wisdom pouring from Sri Yukteswar's lips. His public speeches emphasized the value of *Kriya Yoga,* and a life of self-respect, calmness, determination, simple diet, and regular exercise.

Today, we may mark this day individually, keeping our appointment with God and opening ourselves to the upliftment available on this special date.

Jai Gurus, Victory to those great spiritual masters who have blazed the sadhana trail ahead of us, and even now bless us with their spiritual power of realization.

September 25

TESTED AYURVEDA METHODS

I have incorporated a few Ayurvedic Traditions into my morning routine for some time now (a few for many years), all with good results; I thought I would share these methods with you. Ayurveda (Life-knowledge) is an ancient Hindu medical system that has some easy-to-apply practices. These practices I describe below are supported by many modern studies to be health enhancing.

Tongue Scraping. There are small u-shaped instruments sold for tongue scraping, however you can use a small stainless-steel spoon as well. Lightly scrape the tongue from the back to the front of the mouth. You will get a white/gray substance (brown or green are possible) that contains oral bacteria. Its removal reduces bad breath, increases flavors of foods, can boost the immune system by removing harmful toxins, removes bacteria and toxins that lead to periodontal problems, and is said to activate agni (fire element) that will aid digestion.

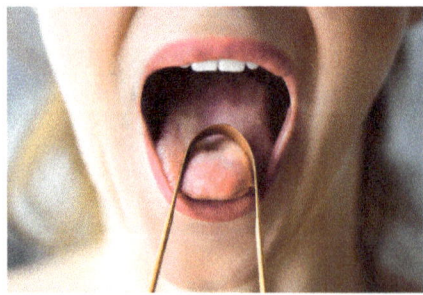

Tongue scraper.**

Neti Pot: I use a ceramic neti pot (that looks a bit like Aladdin's Lamp) filled with salt water (I like the Himalayan Institute neti pot design). The neti pot fits into one nostril, while you tilt your head at a 45-degree angle and the water pours from the top nostril through the nasal passage and out the lower nostril. If you tip your head too far back, it will run down your throat and make you cough. A little practice and you will find the right angle to pour. After pouring the water through the nostrils blow out the excess water. Mainstream medicine has adopted its use for those who have had operations on the nose, and studies have shown those who suffer allergies get relief by this method. This method loosens mucus and allows the cilia to work more efficiently. I buy a premixed saline solution and add water.[34]

Neti pot.**

Oil Pulling: Oil pulling is swishing oil in your mouth for some minutes and then spitting it out into the garbage (not down the sink). Studies have shown that oil pulling helps prevents gingivitis and bad breath by binding

---

34   You are encouraged to do your own research for the best water to utilize.

microorganisms in the mouth and removing them. I use coconut oil (sesame and sunflower oils are ok too), as coconut oil has lauric acid which is an anti-microbial; it also tastes better than the other oils (even though you are not swallowing it). There are various times for swishing recommended, anywhere from 5 minutes to 20 minutes. I have a routine where I am swishing and jogging on the rebounder; the result is I keep the oil in for about 15 minutes. An added benefit may be that you notice your teeth are whiter. A Kriyaban reported their dentist said that the people he sees with the best oral hygiene are those who do oil pulling.

Walking/jogging/running: While not Ayurvedic, part of my morning routine fits in well with Master's recommendation for walking for five minutes and then running for five minutes. I spend ten minutes on the rebounder (a small trampoline). The additional benefit of the rebounder is its healthy effect on the lymphatic system and getting rid of toxins from the body.

You may like to try one or all the above methods for enhancing your health.

Om Namaste Om, I bow to the good and compassionate Creator.

October 9

THE DEPTH OF THIS MYSTERY
KNOWS NO BOUNDS

Krishna with Flute, painting by B. K. Mitra.**

The path of a yogi is suited to the individuality of the practitioner. Only through deep understanding may you know for certain that you are following the highest path. Even then, the notion that you will know everything in a factual sense is never true. What you do know is your absolute oneness with God. You may take on the role of a master, a lover of God, a servant, a child, an instrument, or other such divine expressions. However, what is consistent in all of these spiritual manifestations is the

252 DISCOURSES—VOLUME ONE, 2013–2014

experience that God is the operator of the machine; you are but
the machine. Even what sort of expression you become is according to His will. In this sense, there is no free will, even though
your experience is that of choosing to do His will. Relationships
such as a Father and a Son, a Hand in the glove, the master and
servant, have all joined and merged, one into the other. Now God
and His devotee are interchangeable; it is God who has become
the servant, and the servant has become God. The depth of this
mystery knows no bounds.

October 11

THE WISDOM OF SRI RAMAKRISHNA

Sri Ramakrishna, 1883.

Quote from The Gospel of Sri Ramakrishna:

The feeling of "I and mine" has covered Reality. Because of this we do not see Truth. Attainment of Chaitanya, Divine Consciousness, is not possible without the knowledge of Advaita, Non-duality. After realizing Chaitanya, one enjoys Nityananda, Eternal Bliss. One enjoys this Bliss after attaining the state of a paramhansa.

Do you know what the vision of Divine Consciousness is like? It is like the sudden illumination of a dark room when a match is struck.

The Incarnation of God is accepted by those who follow the path of bhakti. A woman belonging to the Kartabhaja sect observed my condition and remarked: "You have inner realization. Don't dance and sing too much. Ripe grapes must be preserved carefully in cotton. The mother-in-law lessens her daughter-in-law's activities when the daughter-in-law is with child. One characteristic of God-realization is that the activities of a man with such realization gradually drop away. Inside the man [meaning Sri Ramakrishna] is the real Jewel."

Watching me eat, she remarked, "Sir, are you yourself eating, or are you feeding someone else?"

The feeling of ego has covered Truth. Narendra once said, "As the 'I' of man recedes, the 'I' of God approaches." Kadar says, "The more clay there is in the jar, the less water it holds."

Krishna said to Arjuna: "Brother, you will not realize Me if you possess even one of the eight siddhis [powers]." These give only a little power. With healing and the like one may do only a little good to others. Isn't that true?

Therefore, I prayed to the Divine Mother for pure love only, a love that does not seek any return. I never asked for occult powers.

While talking thus, Sri Ramakrishna went into samadhi. He sat there motionless, completely forgetful of the outer world. Then, coming down to the sense world, he sang:

"Ah, friend! I have not found Him yet, whose love has driven me mad . . ."[35]

---

35   *The Gospel of Sri Ramakrishna* (p. 233).

October 12

SWAMI SATCHIDANANDAJI'S MAHASMADHI DAY

Yogacharya David and
Swami Satchidanandaji, 1998.

Dear Swami Muktanandaji and all dear friends,
Today we concluded our meditation service with a tribute to our dear Swami Satchidanandaji and distributed Ashram Prasad packets. Each day I see Swamiji's prominent picture here, given to us by Larryji and Cate. Whenever I think of our dear Swamiji, love and gratitude fill my heart. This fullness of heart is the greatest tribute I can think to bestow upon this precious soul. The year 2008 seems so long ago, but when I think of Swamiji, he feels so close.

We wish to send you our love and gratitude not only for our dear Swamiji, but for all of you at Anandashram who are holding aloft the Light that Swamiji manifested in all that he did. Our Gurudev never tired of saying that out of all there at the ashram; when she went through the terrific experiences of the Mystical

Crucifixion Papa put her through, she felt, above all others there, Swamiji exhibited the most understanding and compassion for her; I know he and Mother always had a special connection. She would with great affection refer to him privately as "Satch."

Such are the thoughts we are having on this special Mahasamadhi Day for our dear Swamiji. Etched forever in my mind is the last time we took our leave from him. I asked if I would see him again in the body, and he answered, "Not likely." Oh, how my heart heaved with grief in that moment. However, for the sake of knowing him, and loving him, I would gladly bear such utter grief a million, million times; for he is my savior and forever I will bow at his feet in gratitude.

Om Sri Ram Jai Ram Jai Jai Ram,
YOGACHARYA DAVID (the name he gave to me)

October 14

SWAMI SATCHIDANANDA'S MAHASAMADHI RESPONSE BY SWAMI MUKTANANDAJI

Swami Muktanandaji and Yogacharya David, 2013.

Revered Davidji,
    Your most loving and touching email, convey-ing your love and gratitude for our Revered and Beloved Swamiji, is heart-rending [and] at the same time, soul-elevating. The last few days have been bringing back all the memories of our dear Swamiji. His love, his forti-tude, his guru-seva, concern for all and his tireless service for all devotees. All we can do is bow our head with grati-tude at HIS Holy Feet and seek HIS blessings to be able to live up to all these noble ideals that He has placed before us through HIS life.

Yes, when we think about it 6 years seems a very long time, but when we think about Pujya Swamiji He is right before us, still looking at us with all the compassion and love in HIS eyes.

A lot of devotees from various places were here for Pujya Swamiji's Maha Samadhi day. The day went off with intense God-remembrance.

Deepest love and best wishes to you, Carlaji, Larry, Cateji, Jillji and all there.

Ever your Self
SWAMI MUKTANANDA

October 16

AWAKE—THE LIFE OF YOGANANDA

Paramhansa Yogananda with
lecture poster in Boston, 1920s.**

"Compelling . . . Enough to make a modern soul look inwards."
—*New York Times* movie review.

I t was an evening spent with many from our Spiritual Group,
dinner at a delightful Asian restaurant, and then on to a much
anticipated movie, *Awake—The Life of Yogananda*, a newly
released movie to a limited number of theaters, and in the case
of Bellingham, for one night only (although they have now scheduled another night in November after a sold out performance

last night). In a word, a wonderfully made film about our beloved param-guru.

With astounding vintage still pictures and moving pictures of Master, Sri Yukteswarji, Anandamayi Ma, and others, the movie makers worked magic with older photos and film to make us feel that we were there. There were a few voice recordings of Master and quotes from Master read by an actor as a voice over, many interviews from some who knew Master and some who were placed in the movie because they are well-known today.

The movie was respectfully and lovingly done; the copyright at the end indicated that it is an SRF production and they own the rights. There are some things I would have preferred. For instance, there was little or none of Master's music performed by him or others, and there were noticeable absences of known recordings and videos by disciples of Master, such as Roy Eugene Davis, Bob Raymer, Yogacharya Black or Yogacharya Mother Hamilton.

The stories told did, somewhat surprisingly, bring out some of the more difficult times in Master's life: the painful separation between Master and Dhirananda, the "yellow journalism" attacks on Master (at least in part due to racism), and his experiences in Washington DC where he was received by the President and his lectures were attended by congressmen and senators, but people of color were not allowed to attend his lectures (Master conducted classes for people of color separately).

The movie told Master's story in such a way that you felt you could actually meet him and know what he would be like, not an "ivory tower" version of him. Overall, an excellent effort in bringing out the life and teachings of Master that is informative and entertaining for all audiences, not just ardent disciples and followers of Master's teachings.

October 24

CHRISTINE: ONE-YEAR ANNIVERSARY

Christine Baldigara, Anandashram, 2007.

Today marks the one-year anniversary of when Christine left the body. What stands out clearly is that when a soul leaves this earthly existence, it leaves a void that cannot be filled by anything or anyone: life is simply not the same, nor will it ever be. As this realization deepens in me, it makes me more aware of how sacred life is; every life, everywhere. That search for the sacred, for divine healing, was such a prominent feature in Christine, and what she inspired in many, many others.

Last night we held a Service for Christine, reading from *The Resurrection of Sri Yukteswar*. I spoke, we then chanted and held silence. While in silence, I beheld Christine in a striking inner vision: She was near a large waterfall; there were lush flowers and foliage all around; all was lit with a beautiful, spring-like sun and peace rang in the air.

We communed in thought and in Spirit. My consciousness expanded like a geyser of radiance, transporting her into higher, more expanded awareness. As beautiful as the astral worlds are, they pale into insignificance in contrast to an experience in over-arching Spirit.

Then for some time, we were again next to the waterfall. She exuded light and a brilliant smile. She indicated that she would wish me to pass on her love to all, and for no one to feel sorry for her, that she is happy and free of bodily pain and restrictions. The feeling of light and happiness comes easily and joyfully as I think of her now.

How I started writing about Christine and what I have just now written seem to be two realities, a physical one in which Christine has left a void of absence, and a spiritual reality in which she is ever-present and shining in a new world. Both are true, and while we deeply miss her, the greater reality is her eternal exis-tence in God. This is the key to all healing around the physical death of a loved one; while acknowledging the loss, we may also know the eternal existence of the Soul.

What stands out to me in this moment is the tremendous feel-ing of love in my heart in thinking about Christine. A feeling of fulfillment, that what she strove for in life, spiritual healing, has come to pass. Christine now has freedom from fear and has found joy—freedom from aloneness and separation—and is joined into oneness in Spirit. She has freedom from disappointment and is content in Divine Love, and now she has a playground of all astral creation that more easily accommodates her vast desire to create beauty!

She earned all of these spiritual gifts by her relentless striving while here. Christine courageously faced her past demons, some-times shaking and shuddering in the process, but never turning away from her path. And her expansive heart ever wanted to include everyone in the experience of growth, for she believed in, and eventually came to know, the real freedom and the lasting happiness that comes with bravely facing darkness in order to know the Light. This courage and tenacity for growth is what stands like a monument in Christine for all to emulate and follow.

October 28

YOUR HEART'S DESIRE

Sri Yukteswar.**

Awake at 1 a.m., worries about money come unbidden to mind, "How am I going to pay my bills? How can I ever go on vacation? My old car needs to be replaced: how can I ever do that? My business is stalled, money is going out the window, I am more and more in debt!"

Awake at 7 a.m. "Oh, another day. I am so lonely. What is wrong with me that I do not have someone special in my life? I want someone to especially love, and who will love me! I just want to roll over and go back to sleep; there I may feel some respite from this loneliness."

Just two examples of how we worry and cry bucket loads of tears about our unfilled desires. Is it so inconceivable that you would cry over not knowing God? That you would remain awake, thinking that days, years are going by and you do not know God, or deeply love Him? That you would wake in the night, wondering how you will pay for the air that you breathe?

What if you yearned for God at least as much as you desire things in this world? What if you worried if you will know God as your complete lover as much as you yearn to be loved by that someone special in your life?

At one point in my life, I started to connect the idea that all my desires for things and satisfaction found in this world was really my desire for God. Sri Yukteswarji quoted the Vedas, saying that God is the fulfillment of all your heart's desires. Just think, everything you desire, everything you worry about, everything that causes you stress in this world, it is all satisfied through your connection with the Divine Presence.

Begin today by transferring your allegiance, your focus of attention, and your love to God and not the world. You will still live in the world. Therefore, you must give it its due. However, inwardly, deeply, you look to God as your all and all, in all. Discover that amazingly, simply, your heart's desire and fulfillment is, and always has been, right within you.

November 5

GOD IS YOUTHFULNESS ITSELF

Baby Krishna hugging Swami Satchidananda,
drawing by Gargi (Lakshmi), Anandashram.**

Monday, we had Skype Service with the Ashland Group, and as I spoke, deeper levels of Truth were unfolding in my mind from the great Mind. The topic was Eternal Youth. We used Master's *Is Everlasting Youth Possible?* to understand how mind controls the atoms of the body. The additional layer that came so clear to me was that the Fountain of Youth that Ponce de Leon sought, and down through history mankind has sought, is to be found right within.

I am sure Ponce thought of finding some magical spring water that would keep him in a youthful body and death far away. However, the *youthfulness* God was showing me had less to do with the body and more to do with the Spirit. **Contacting God is youthfulness itself**. The Self is always youthful in spirit.

When we see a baby or a little child smiling, playing and being charming, we are reminded of our original innocence, that part of us that has not grown old in the world. In that moment, we feel love, the joy of eternal Spirit, bubbling up from some unbidden Source within. Being with the world too much makes us old, wary and grief stricken. Being with God makes us young, brimming with life-force and enthusiasm for what God is going to bring us next.

Surely you have been given tasks to do in this world, and there are times that, like a bridge bearing a large load, you can creek and groan. However, even when life seems to be straining you, even then you may feel true joy. The secret is to remain identified with the Self. Stepping back from the challenge, observe the movie of this life from the projectionist booth with God at your side. "Fine joke, Ram! Look where you have put me now. Surely You mean well. You, must guide me and show me the way through."

Then you feel God smile. You feel a fresh spring air blow through you and you feel lighter, optimistic, and secure. The thought of Krishna comes to mind; he is smiling even when calamitous events are unfolding. Why is he smiling? Because he sees the Big Picture, not just the little frames of individual incidents. The Big Picture tells him that all is occurring exactly as it ought to, and that all is working for the highest good of all.

To be aware of the loving Hand that controls and guides all events in creation breathes new life into you, makes you young again. And, as Master points out, mind controls the atoms of the body. With the mind merged in the Infinite, then the healing salve of health, youthfulness, and inner knowing that all is well must be in residence, for body mind and soul.

November 12

SWAMI SATCHIDANANDA'S BIRTHDAY

Yogacharya David and Swami Satchidananda, Anandashram, 2007.

T oday is Swami Satchidananda's birthday. When I originally went to Anandashram, I viewed the time I would
spend there as an ideal setting for spiritual practice. What
I did not know beforehand was the tremendous impact Swami
Satchidananda would have on me and on my search for God.

I have since come to regard Swamiji as my Second Mother. His
placid mien, quiet sense of humor, and soft-spoken words were
so different in expression than my first Mother, my gurudev.

However, in essentials he was very much the same as Mother
Hamilton. Inner steel underlies the calm exterior, passion for
God and Gurus drove him mercilessly, and in the end, spiritual

enlightenment informed every word and action that naturally emanated from him.

Birthdays are for acknowledging a soul taking incarnation. Surely the highest attainment for a soul in life is to realize God. Swamiji achieved that great goal, and in addition, he inspired thousands to have the utmost integrity in their search for God, settling for nothing less than the highest union with God.

My life would have been incomplete without my dear Swamiji, unimaginable. With complete love and reverence, I bow at his feet. Thank you Swamiji for all that you have done and continue to do in my life, and in the lives of so many.

Quote of the Day: Anandashram

Our main object in life must be to realise the truth of our oneness with God and thereby enjoy eternal happiness. For this purpose, intense Sadhana is necessary. In the course of Sadhana, usually we may not be able to spend all the 24 hours in meditation. It may be necessary for us to devote some time, or in some cases, more time in useful service. Useful service means whatever work we do should be done looking upon it as service to God. This is actually divinising all activities. This practice will help our Sadhana and hence, the activities do not become a hindrance to our Sadhana and prayers.[36]

—SWAMI SATCHIDANANDA

36 www.anandashram.org

November 18

SIMPLE LIVING AND HIGH THINKING
AND THE GOLDEN MIDDLE PATH

Buddha statue at Bhubaneswar, India.**

There are those who associate a spiritual path with suffering, deprivations, and living in a cave. Surely there have been saints both in the East and the West who have followed in such a style. However, Lahiri Mahasaya, Master, and Mother demonstrated that living in a cave is not the only way to realization.

Surely being driven by greed, with money as your god, does not lead to realization. And living in poverty does not necessarily

promote saintliness, but rather leaves a hunger and need unsatis-
fied. As the Buddha taught, there is a golden middle path.

A person's circumstances will help determine what that middle
path looks like. Generally, as householders, we require a house
to live in. If you are employed in this world, you need the instruments that allow you that life: a car, phone, the right clothes, a
computer, and so on. If your work in the world is such that you
need to entertain, you may have a larger home for that purpose.
In other words, your needs determine what possessions you have.

However, in this world, material belongings make demands
upon us in thought, energy, money, and maintenance. Even something kept in a closet requires something from you. Proof of this
is when you let go of a possession that has secretly lived in a
closet for years, you feel relief and freedom when it is gone.

It is important that your needs and your possessions are in the
right proportion to your life. Master used to say, "Simple living
and high thinking." Simple living and high thinking mean that your
possessions are right sized to your needs, and your thoughts are
upon God and upon being of service to this world. When you
have mastered this balance, you will feel harmony with your sur-
roundings, and you will know a sense of freedom that no material
wealth can ever give you.

Sri Yukteswarji emphasized that being methodical and well
organized needs to be a part of any plan for simple living. I am
still learning this lesson; however, I definitely see the wisdom in
mastering it. For instance, when traveling it is best to limit yourself to the basics; oftentimes, I over-pack and I then pay the price
for it. Planning ahead, having a calm mind, and being methodical
certainly pay off when packing for a trip, and for traveling in life.

At times I would love to live in the simplicity of a cave; however, my life demands more than that. The golden middle path is
elusive, but I work to find that balance and stay on it!

I invite you to be on the journey with me. Perhaps you have traveled ahead of me in this area of being organized and stream-lined. When I see examples of those of you who have this quality, I take note and seek to learn more. When I enquire how this is done, what I hear is there is ruthlessness in getting rid of things no longer needed. I am determined to be as simple as my needs in life allow.

Let simple living and high thinking be our mantra for finding the golden middle path. Like the musician who, unknowingly, was the teacher of the Buddha when he told his student, "Do not over-tighten the stringed instrument or it will break, and do not allow it to be too loose or it will not make the proper sound." Continuously work to find the right balance in your life and then feel the freedom promised in the golden middle path of simple living and high thinking.

November 27

GIVING THANKS

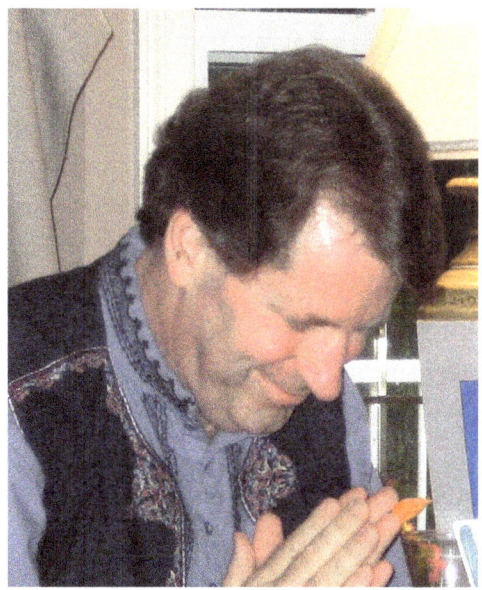

Yogacharya David, 2012.**

Thanksgiving has been a hallowed and cultural tradition for many years now. Times of thanksgiving, prayer, and fasting have been part of American tradition from before its inception.

When the pilgrims arrived, they were poorly prepared for the harsh winter in their new colony. Without the help of Squanto, a sole survivor of the Patuxet Tribe, who showed the new arrivals survival skills, such as how to catch eel, plant corn, and was an interpreter with the nearby tribes, the Pilgrims would have been far worse off.

After their first year and a successful harvest, the 50 surviving Pilgrims (out of the original 100) invited a neighboring tribe, the Wampanoags, to a thanksgiving celebration. Their chief, Massasoit, had supplied precious food the previous winter for the starving colonists. Massasoit arrived with 90 warriors. Fortunately, they brought game with them to supplement the supplies of the colonists; the four surviving adult women supervised the cooking for the three-day feast!

During the revolutionary days, it was not unusual to have a nationwide day of fasting and prayer to commemorate a battle and provide spiritual strength for gaining independence. George Washington declared a day of Thanksgiving in gratitude for the birth of a revolutionary idea, a constitutional government.

This tradition was continued by presidents down to the Civil War. In the midst of the war, Abraham Lincoln declared a nationwide day of Thanksgiving for all the blessings, even in the middle of a terrible war. It was intended to come toward the end of the year, giving thanks for all that was good in the year.

And that idea of setting aside a day for giving thanks has continued. A day for gratitude. My first thought of gratitude is for the general lack of wars in this world. While we work for a world free of all conflicts and fights, it is good to acknowledge that the bitter past has been replete with terrible death and destruction as nation has fought against nation. Today, thankfully, there are no major wars.

The next point of gratitude is for the plentiful supply of food. Times past have seen widespread famines and lack that made hunger a daily pain. Again, it is relative, but today the world has a plentiful supply, if not evenly distributed. This is a good for which I give thanks.

My list would continue for friends, family, and much more, but the last and most important on my list of thankfulness is for my spiritual life. My gratitude goes out to those pioneering souls who surrendered all at the feet of God and whose lives have made our spiritual path possible.

From Jesus and Babaji, to Lahiri Mahasaya, Sri Yuketswarji, Master, and Mother, as well as Swami Ramdas, Mother Krishnabai, Swami Satchidananda, and the multitude of truly worshipful saints and realized beings down the ages, I give humble thanks for the lives they led, the teachings they generously imparted, and the truly superior examples of their lives. They dedicated their lives and their all to the upliftment and enlightenment of this world.

And to you my friends, God has given us each other that we may support each other in gaining the highest attainment in the realization of our oneness with God, and for serving one another with love. For you my heart overflows with love and thanksgiving. May you be blessed with all the good that life has to offer, and most of all, to experience the Divine Presence, within and without.

November 30

DIVINE RESCUE

Grace of the Divine Mother.**

You might say this is about anti-thanksgiving, those things we are not grateful for: when people lie, cheat, steal, and even murder. As aspirants for realization, what do we do when our lives are touched by, or we collide with, such situations?

There will be few who have not done any of these things themselves; and fewer still whose lives have not been seriously disturbed by others who do. We must have an avenue to get through such times so that we do no harm to ourselves or others "and so" that we may actually do what we can to set the situation right.

When it comes to my own behavior, I act as if all that I do will be used as headlines in the newspaper or television. This can have a sobering effect on any misbehavior. It is interesting that when I have done something wrong, I have wanted it to be done in secret.

Knowing that to God, all of His angels, and the spiritual Masters there are no secrets, there is no place to hide and everything is known, then only a fool can believe no one will know. Jesus said it most graphically when he said, That which you think you do in secret will be shouted from the rooftops!

When your life is touched by others who lie, cheat, and steal, there can be no doubt that you will have some reaction. Mother Hamilton, in her fully realized state, said that others imagine that she could not feel hurt or pain because of someone else's actions or words. She said that was most assuredly not true; she could feel deeply hurt.

So, what distinguishes a realized soul from those of us in spiritual ignorance? The difference is that such hurt did not separate Mother from her conscious oneness with God; for others it does, and that makes all the difference.

And it is in this difference that you can find a stepping stone to freedom. When someone injures you through misbehavior, you see the situation as you imagine God would see it. You may think, God feels pain for everyone involved, but He is also dispassionate; God is always God. And God always sees the truth of a situation, He is not blinded by a need to gloss over a behavior.

By mentally staying connected to God, you remain anchored to your vast, Divine Nature, even while you interact with the pain and disappointment of this world. Highly realized souls can feel deep pain by what others do. Master went to Mexico after a betrayal by a childhood friend and helper in his work here in America, feeling that he just wanted to return to India, until

Divine Mother prompted him to stay and complete his work in America.

A touching experience occurred during Sri Yukteswar's last days on earth when he had a deep disappointment, although it did not include wrong behavior. It happened when he had asked Master to stay with him, but Yoganandaji was keen upon attending the Kumbha Mela where he hoped to have the darshan of Babaji. When Sri Yukteswar came to know that Master had left, he took to bed for three days in a deep despair.

It can be disturbing to know that great spiritual masters can be affected by others, but it can be comforting as well. The key to finding your way through a situation is whether you take your mind off God or you keep your attention upon the One. You may still feel pain, distress, anger, and frustration, but with a perfected consciousness there is not a cloud of separation from the light of God; in fact, your mind goes deeper into God, such as Lahiri Mahasaya did when he came to know he was to soon leave the body.

This is something to deeply think upon during this time of Thanksgiving. When God is present in disappointment and tragedy, then pearls of Truth may be realized and the great Comforter may come to you in a dark night; these rescues from the Divine are truly something to be thankful for.

December 2

FROM ADDICTION TO FREEDOM

Jesus knocking on the door, from fresco
painting in Herz Jesu Church, early 1900s.**

There are so many kinds of addictions in this world: alcohol, drugs, sex, gambling, anger, and eating are among the most common. The brain and biochemistry are powerful actors; some will say they are everything. And yet there are those who rise above these addictions and genetic predispositions, those who choose a course of freedom.

The pain of addiction is tremendous, affecting the lives of not only those with the addiction, but the lives they touch, and in turn the lives those people touch, in a ripple effect that spreads out in all directions. Support of family, individual will, and faith in God are typical antidotes thought of to abstain from addiction.

For many, these factors turn the tide, yet, in too many cases these usual formulas are not enough. The family is supportive, the individual deeply wants to change, and he or she prays to God for relief, yet the addiction continues.

Just as the biochemistry of individuals vary, so too may the prescription for recovery. What is common to all abstention from addictions is a clarity in the individual's mind for the damage created by the addiction, a clear, unambiguous desire to be free of the addiction, and a concrete course of action for gaining this freedom.

This course of action may be a 12-step program, aversion therapy, counseling, and so on. The key is that there must be a commitment, the right kind of support, clarity regarding the damage, and an unwavering desire to be free.

To some it may sound surprising that faith in God alone cannot solve the problem. There are those for whom an internal connection with God is exactly right, while others must look to God's helping hand being extended through a specific program.

There is an instructive story about a man who is warned that a flood is threatening his home and he must evacuate. The man thinks, "I have faith in God. He will see to my safety." The flood waters rise up to his porch. A four-wheel drive truck comes by and the driver tells the man to get in the truck and he will take him to safety. The man waves off the driver, telling him to save others, God will take care of him. Then the flood waters rise up and the first story of his house is now underwater. A motorboat pulls up and offers the man a ride to dry land. Again, he waves off the rescuers, secure that God will keep him safe.

Finally, the man is standing on his chimney; his house is covered by the rising flood when a helicopter flies overhead and lowers a harness. The man waves off the helicopter when suddenly he is swept away and drowns.

Arriving at St. Peter's gate soaking wet, he asks to talk directly with God. He is escorted in to an interview with the Almighty, dripping river water on His carpet. "God, why didn't you save me?" he asks with irritation. God looks the man in the eye, "Look, I gave you advance warning, then I sent you a truck, and a boat, and finally a helicopter. You refused all of these. What else could I do?"

We must be willing to humbly accept the help that God sends us, and with a clear determination, to never give up striving for freedom! Even if it is with our last breath in life and we continue to strive for freedom, we will carry that determination with us into our new existence.

December 9

PREPARING FOR A TENDER BIRTH

Adoration of the Shepherds, painting by
Bartolome Esteban Murillo, 17th Century.**

The approach of Christmas is oftentimes ascribed to be a stressful season, and surely it is a time that can be jammed-packed with activities and demands. However, for many years I observed in my spiritual life, and now the lives of many others, that there is an additional layer of why this can be a difficult time.

The winter solstice occurs on or near December 21st. The solstice marks the shortest day of sunlight due to the earth's tilt and its rotation around the sun. It has long been noted that celestial movements relate to changes in consciousness, and from this observation, astrology had its origins. The winter solstice and its opposite, the summer solstice, as well as the two equinoxes, have special relevance to inner changes as well as the more obvious outer changes.

Since meeting my guru and my subsequent initiation, I noticed that the time preceding the winter solstice was oftentimes difficult, stirring up much mental and emotional turmoil. In the beginning, I associated this fact with the holidays making me more acutely aware that I was alone.

As the seasons rolled by, I noticed that this intensity in the buildup climaxed, not with Christmas, but, with the solstice itself. With the solstice, the intensity would "break," and the immediate days before Christmas were much easier, very enjoyable. Year after year, I noticed the same pattern, and once seen it could not be unseen.

It is no accident that the birth of Jesus is marked at this time of year. Symbolically it is the depth of darkness and the beginning of the procession to the light: a perfect time for the birth of the "Light of the world" to incarnate. Historians tell us that for the shepherds to be out tending their flocks at night, as depicted in the scriptures, it would be springtime, lambing season. So, December would not be the historical birth date of Jesus, but March or April. However, not only is the end of December symbolically right, but the intense purification before the solstice followed by uplifting joy is the perfect time for the birth of the savior.

When we understand that this increasing intensity is part of a purification rite, and its purpose is the birth of something new, then we can consciously cooperate with this progression, understand it, and receive the greatest benefits from its annual occurrence.

Rejoice, for something wonderful is coming! Prepare the way and spread your wings so that the seasonal uplifting currents will carry you heavenward; listen carefully and you will hear the celestial music of the spheres. The tender birth of the Christ-child is coming; the ancient prophesies are to be fulfilled right within your own being.

December 11

AN AGENT OF TRUTH,
STRENGTH, AND HEALING

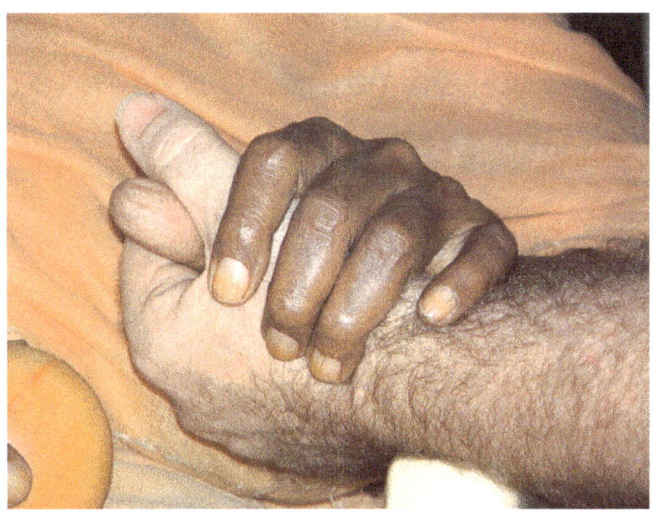

Yogacharya David and Swami Satchidananda, 2007.**

ragedy comes into the home in many ways. Sickness and Death are two common ways, but there are also tragedies of stealing, lying, cruel words, domestic violence, and silent withholding. These are some familiar tragedies that too often snake their way into the home. While the first two instances may be beyond our direct control, the later acts are volitional and entirely within our choosing.

There are those who unthinkingly perpetuate such pain on a daily basis, many times without really thinking of the effect it has on others. I remember many years ago when I was in my master's degree program, we were enacting an adult student's childhood family situation at Christmas time. She chose me to play her father, and two good friends of mine played her brothers. In this scenario, there were common verbal fights and occasional drunken brawls that broke out to commemorate the season of "brotherly love and goodwill toward all mankind."

I made a startling discovery in re-enacting the verbal fight; I felt the power of anger and loud, aggressive words pouring out of me. Then I was replaced by the woman whose family we represented; now I was a witness only. The difference in the effect this clash had on me, based on my perspective, was stark. I felt the loud words going right through me; I was physically assaulted by the vibrational violence. Where before I felt in control, now there was no sense of control and that anything might happen.

I was stunned by this change of perspective; it made me realize that many of those who yell, swear, threaten, and possibly get violent have little idea of the effect they have on others. The one who is yelling knows what he or she will do or not do, while others are left to imagine to what extent it can all go.

When doing family therapy, I have oftentimes thought how useful it would be to videotape the session, so that others may hear how they sound, and see what they look like when interacting with others. For many, it would be shocking to hear his or her own tone of voice and see the look on their face.

Self-awareness is the first step in making a change. You can make more of an effort at self-awareness by really observing yourself in any situation. When you evaluate that what you say, or how you say it, is not reflective of the person you want to be, then get busy and change your behavior. Simply writing it off as, "This is just the way I am," is the coward's way and will lead to intense future regrets.

Make sure that your words are sweet, so just in case you have to "eat your words," well, you get the picture! Make your goal in life for every thought, word, and action to be an expression of your highest Self, then you will not have to live with regret ever again. You are now an agent of truth, strength, and healing for yourself and for all.

December 18

THE POWER BEHIND THE ATOM AND ALL CREATION

The Helix Nebula.

I sit in inner stillness; a tremendous pressure is in the base of my skull. I focus inside this intense pain; the sound of Aum/Amen is remarkably loud. My vision goes into the center of this dense power; I see the "atoms" inside this density, what appears to me now as so many galaxies in a vast universe. The compact density expands, the pressure in my head reduces, and the feeling of power increases, only now it is spread out over vast space.

There is so much power behind creation, inside the cell, an atom, and even a quark; it is all the power of creation itself. Dumb power could not create out of randomness all that we see about us. I perceive this great intelligence and beauty in this power; to perceive this vision is awe-inspiring.

This mystical experience is the remover of fear and the birth of Christ Consciousness. The microcosm and the macrocosm are not different but are expressions of the one power. This is a mystery to the uninitiated, and self-evident to those who know.

The holy birth is here, it is now, and it is ever-present.

December 23

COME INTO MY KINGDOM

Gifts of pictures by Lillian Grace.

The last of the devotees depart after a weekend of celebrating Christmas with our spiritual family. The house is quiet, and yet not quiet, for the all-powerful sound of Aum/Amen is ringing in the air, and from the walls, floor, and ceiling. My heart is full and complete.

God is the *special ingredient* that makes for this total contentment. All the plans could look the same: Christmas carols the night before, spiritual service followed by a potluck, a social gathering of such wonderful souls, but without the vibration of God, the festivities would be incomplete, an unnamed emptiness.

But with God, oh, what a different story! Upon meeting each person, my heart is an overflowing cup of love, the eyes flow with bliss, the Soul is touched, and a depth of Spirit is reached that makes the world bright and peaceful. The Divine ingredient makes it all sacred. It is the true philosopher's stone that turns all it touches into gold; the gold of the Spirit.

For so many years, I yearned for this and did not have it. How many lonely Christmases, how much time was spent living in separation, knowing there was more, like the waif on the outside, in the cold, watching those on the inside share a warm banquet. I keenly felt the Divine absence.

Now the Infinite Presence lives in my heart and soul; separation is but a memory of the past. Oh, how I long to have all yearning souls share in the Kingdom, to know that through total surrender comes spiritual perfection.

Come my dear ones; come into the kingdom of bliss, light, and peace. Come, oh blessed Christ, come! By whatever the name you may call upon the one, the redeemer of mankind; for it is through Thy Grace that all are lifted, even on this day, into the waiting Kingdom of Spirit.

I continue listening to the resounding Aum coming from everywhere and nowhere, and I know that it is the result of God's Presence combined with all the wonderful souls who have celebrated this holy season with us today. And this feeling, this music of Spirit, this is the best Christmas gift I could ever hope to receive. It is the vibrancy of the Holy Ghost and Christ Consciousness born anew, manifesting through this blissful sound. And its words sing through the very cells of my Being: Merry Christmas to you, and goodwill toward all!

December 25

MAGIC IN THE AIR

Yogacharya David's first Christmas. David (center)
with his brothers Jerry and Mark, 1954.**

hristmas Eve: For a child, there is such magic in the air in anticipation of what is to come in the morning. We perpetuate the story of Santa Claus because we love that same feeling, for children and for ourselves. Why? Because it stirs something deep, wonderful, and beautiful inside.

Later in life, we learn the unreality of it all, and something diminishes inside. That is until we see the wide-eyed wonder in a child in anticipation of the magic. What is it in us that so yearns for magic? It is the intuitive faculty within that yearns for God.

God is that feeling of magic, of charm, of an open field of possibilities, and of joy and love. To feel the openness of anticipation means a beautiful world of splendor awaits us. Being overly mind-ful of the "realism" of life kills in us this awareness; it removes the childlike wonder.

Jesus said that children are blessed, because a childlike nature is part of entering into heaven. The master actually thanks God for not revealing heaven to the intellectual and prideful, but rather to the childlike in spirit. Jesus and his disciples were living in a tough existence; he was no starry-eyed dreamer, his world could scarce afford that. Rather, his affirmation of innocence as necessary is a statement of a tremendous truth. We must be open to wonder, to the incredible beauty in which we can look at a lily of the field and find greatness.

Some may scoff at such words, but this cynical mindset is exactly what Jesus was thanking God for leaving in ignorance. Blessed are the children, of all ages, for such is the kingdom of heaven.

I am sitting to meditate on Christmas Eve, and I sit in wonder, anticipation of untold possibilities, of magic in the air; for such is the kingdom of God.

December 27

Swami Ramdas' Sannyas Day

Swami Ramdas (Papa) in the Panch
Pandav Cave, Mangalore, India.

Today we mark the anniversary when Swami Ramdas took sannyas, the life of a wandering mendicant. We may all take inspiration from Papa in his complete surrender to God, his fearlessness in throwing his lot in with the inner promptings of his beloved Ram, and the good cheer in which he carried out even the most severe disciplines. Whether God calls us to such a wandering life, or He directs us to some other, the same complete surrender is required to attune our bodies, minds, and souls, not with the lower impulses, but with the highest, most beautiful, sublime states of consciousness available to anyone.

Here is how Papa spoke of that initial change in his life, many years after the fact—Swami Ramdas on Himself:

> The great change came over Ramdas in 1922 with his life of renunciation not as a result of his own effort or initiative, but by the power, Will and grace of God. Until this transformation came to him, he was living only an ordinary life. This does not mean that he was selfish or inflicted any injury upon others or exploited others for his personal happiness. It was only that he was not aware then that there was a great Reality underlying this universal manifestation and that by attaining that Reality one could become supremely happy and peaceful, free from all anger, hate and bickering, which brought him in daily conflict with his fellow-beings.
>
> When this great change came, Ramdas was swept off his feet, as it were. He did not know what was going to happen to him. He was asked to repeat the name of God constantly, to keep his mind serene and calm, so that it could go deeper within himself, to find the truth on which his life was based. For that purpose, he was made to give up everything, all attachments to worldly life, worldly relations, and he was taken from place to place in a state which was really wonderful. In that state he felt neither attraction nor repulsion for the world. The world had practically ceased to exist for him. His mind was merely an instrument in the hands of the Divine and he was being led by that Power. His mind was merged in ineffable peace and bliss.
>
> Having experienced that supreme joy in this state, Ramdas was going about telling everybody that, if they

lived on the lower levels of life like animals, they could never get real happiness. They must transcend all these and go deep down within themselves and realize the all-pervading eternal Spirit, which is pure bliss and peace. In this way for nearly four years, Ramdas was wandering from place to place, and during his wanderings, he was made to remain for days together in caves and jungles in order that he might get the fullness of spiritual experience which is the aim and purpose of human life.[37]

---

37   *Swami Ramdas on Himself* (p. 7).

Conclusion

I Am Your Instrument

Oh Lord—I am Your instrument

For You see through my eyes

And the world shines in splendor

You are the Light of this world.

And I am Your agent

Your love pours through my heart

Like a vast, endless river

And the world is washed clean in Your love.

You painfully break me

And Your compassion issues forth,

It deconstructs this complex world

And salves the world in loving compassion.

Oh Infinite Self

Solo Creator of island universe

You see Your puny human vessel

And fulfil Your boundless purpose.

It is my joy—my greatest joy

To be Your instrument

That You use me as Your pen

To write Your story in the Book of Life.[38]

—Yogacharya David

OM TAT SAT AUM

Mount Temple, Alberta, Canada, painting by Dennis Brown.

---

38   *Climbing the Sacred Mountain: Poems and Prayers of a Western Yogi* (p. 48). A poem from 2013.

References

Arnold, Edwin, Sir. (1905). *The Song Celestial; or, Bhagavad-Gita.* London: Dryden House.

Davis, Roy Eugene. (2005). *Paramhansa Yogananda: As I Knew Him.* Center for Spiritual Awareness, Lakemont, Georgia: CSA Press.

Gupta, Mahendranath. Translator Swami Nikhilananda. (1942). *The Gospel of Sri Ramakrishna.* New York: Ramakrishna-Vivekananda Center.

Hickenbottom, Yogacharya David. (2022). *Silence: Entering the Cosmic Sea of Consciousness.* Camano Island, WA.: The Cross and The Lotus Publishing.

Hickenbottom, Yogacharya David. (2022). *Notes to Sadhakas.* Camano Island, WA.: The Cross and The Lotus Publishing.

Hickenbottom, Yogacharya David. (2021). *Climbing the Sacred Mountain: Poems and Prayers of a Western Yogi.* Camano Island, WA.: The Cross and The Lotus Publishing.

Hickenbottom, Yogacharya David. (2019). *My Spiritual India.* Camano Island, WA.: The Cross and The Lotus Publishing.

Hopko, Thomas, Father. Translator from Russian, Olga Savin. (2001). Foreword. *The Way of a Pilgrim and The Pilgrim Continues His Way.* Boston, Massachusetts: Shambhala Publications, Inc.

Kamala. (1993). *The Flawless Mirror.* Los Angeles, California: Crystal Clarity Publishers.

Paramhansa Prajnananda. (1999). *Swami Shriyukteshwar: Incarnation of Wisdom.* Odisha, India: Prajnana Mission.

Paramhansa Yogananda. (2007). *The Second Coming of Christ*. Los Angeles, California: Self Realization Fellowship.

Paramhansa Yogananda. (1949). *Whispers from Eternity*. Los Angeles, California: Self-Realization Fellowship.

Paramhansa Yogananda. (1946). *Autobiography of a Yogi*. New York: The Philosophical Library.

Paramhansa Yogananda. (1938). *Is Everlasting Youth Possible? Praecepta Lessons*. Vol. 3. Los Angeles, California: Self-Realization Fellowship.

Swami Ramdas. (1984). *Poems*. Kerala, India: Anandashram.

Swami Ramdas. (1984). *Swami Ramdas on Himself*. Kerala, India: Anandashram.

Wells, H.G. (1961). *The Outline of History*. Garden City, New York: Garden City Publishers.

Wright, Richard, C. (1936, November). *Visit with Kara Patri*. News From India. *Inner Culture East-West Magazine, Vol. IX*. Los Angeles, California: Self-Realization Fellowship.

Bible References

King James Bible Online: https//www.kingjamesbibleonline.org

Dictionary: www.Merriam-Webster.com/dictionary/pilgrim

Film References

Awake: The Life of Yogananda. Los Angeles, California: Self-Realization Fellowship. Counterpoint Films with filmmakers Paola di Florio, Lisa Leeman, and Peter Radar.

Mystic India. Produced by BAPS Swaminarayan Sanstha. https//www.mystic india.com

Website References:

Mother Hamilton and Yogacharya David Reference: The Cross and The Lotus: www.crossandlotus.com

Anandashram Reference: www.anandashram.org

Original Christianity Original Yoga: https://ocoy.org/ yoganandas-last-days/

Poem: *My India:* https://aumamen.com/topic/ my-india-a-poem-by-paramahansa-yogananda

Paramhansa Yogananda's Last Speech: https://www.utkalgaurav. org/assets/img/Last%20speech.pdf

Thanksgiving. Smithsonian Magazine: https://www.smithsonianmag. com/blogs/national-museum-american-indian/2016/11/27/ do-american-indians-celebrate-thanksgiving/

Ramakrishna: https://en.wikipedia.org/wiki/Ramakrishna

Image Attribution

With the exception of those listed below, all images are used courtesy of the Yogacharya David and Carla Hickenbottom portfolio. Photos were taken by David and Carla Hickenbottom or gifted with permission by friends, family, and devotees. Attribution for images from these sources has not been included here. Devotees have all given permission for the images or written submissions to be portrayed in this text.

Images listed are available for free use in the public domain, under Creative Commons licensing, or licensed from other sources as noted.

2013 September 29. *Anandamayi Ma* by Richard Lannoy on Anandamayi.org. Public domain.

2013 October 3. *Belur Math* by Saiko3p on Shutterstock.com. License purchased.

2013 October 3. *Sri Ramakrishna* in samadhi during a kirtan at Keshab Sen's house, 1879. *The Gospel of Sri Ramakrishna,* pp. 676–677. Commons.wikimedia.org. Public domain.

2013 October 17. *Swami Chidananda Puri* by Gangaputri on Wikimedia Commons is licensed under CC BY-SA 4.0.

2013 December 24. *The Holy Night* by Carlo Maratta, 17th Century. Public domain.

2013 December 27. *Swami Ramdas at Panch Pandav Cave,* Mangalore, India. 1920s. Anandashram.org. Public domain.

2014 January 10. *Paramhansa Yogananda. The Last Smile* by Arthur Say, 1952. Public domain.

2014 January 14. *Paramhansa Yogananda at Kumbha Mela, Allahabad*, 1936. Public domain.

2014 January 28. *Agony in the Garden* by Franz Schwartz, 1898. Public domain.

2014 February 15. *Divine Mercy of Jesus Sacred Heart* by Prasad KB on Dreamstime.com. License purchased.

2014 March 09. *Sri Yukteswar.* Commons.wikimedia.org. Public domain.

2014 March 10. *Paramhansa Yogananda.* Cover portrait for *Autobiography of a Yogi*, 1946. Public domain.

2014 March 11. *Paramhansa Yogananda* with Luther Burbank. *Autobiography of a Yogi*, p. 345. Public domain.

2014 March 12. *Paramhansa Yogananda Writing.* Commons. wikimedia.org. Public domain.

2014 March 13. *Paramhansa Yogananda with Madam Sen.* Arthur Say. 1952. Public domain.

2014 March 14. *Paramhansa Yogananda The Last Smile* by Arthur Say, 1952. Public domain.

2014 March 15. *Paramhansa Yogananda with Autobiography.* Commons.wikimedia.org. Public domain.

2014 March 16. *Paramhansa Yogananda Playing the Esraj.* Commons.wikimedia.org. 1936. Public domain.

2014 March 22. *Swami Ramdas.* Anandashram.org. Public domain.

2014 September 22. *Paramhansa Yogananda and Sri Yukteswar at Solstice Celebration.* 1935. *Autobiography of a Yogi*, p. 36. Public domain.

2014 September 25. *Tongue Scraper* by Andrey Popov on Dreamstime.com. License purchased.

2014 September 25. *Ceramic Neti Pot* by Beata Jana Filarova on Dreamstime.com. License purchased.

2014 October 09. *Krishna in Brindavana* by B.K. Mitra, undated, Hindi Gita Press Mahabharata on Commons.wikimedia.org. Public domain.

2014 October 11. *Sri Ramakrishna Paramahansa*, 1911. Ramakrishna.org. Public domain.

2014 October 16. *Paramhansa Yogananda*, Boston Massachusetts. Commons.wikimedia.org. Public domain.

2014 November 05. *Krishna with Swami Satchidananda* by Gargi (Lakshmi). Permission granted.

2014 December 02. *Early 1900s Fresco in Herz Jesu Church, Vienna, Austria* by Josef Sedmak on Dreamstime.com. License purchased.

2014 December 09. *Adoration of the Shepherds* by Bartolome Esteban Murillo, 17th Century. Public domain.

2014 December 18. *The Helix Nebula* on Hubblesite.org. Public domain.

2014 December 27. *Swami Ramdas at Panch Pandav Cave*, Mangalore, India, 1920s. Anandashram.org. Public domain.

Conclusion: *Mount Temple*, Alberta, Canada. Painting by Dennis Brown. Permission granted.

Acknowledgments

Yogacharya David has a unique ability to share spiritual teachings and soul-enhancing reflections in a most accessible manner—he can reach us in our day-to-day ways of being as we strive to live a purposeful life. He guides us, and even as he laughs at himself, he still seriously advocates for a wake-up process.

It is a privilege to form what we call Team-David, a dedicated team of aspirants who willingly devote time and expertise to ensuring that Yogacharya David's legacy of teachings reach those who long for a deeper, broader, and disciplined-yet-freeing approach to life's journey.

Carla Hickenbottom, David's wife and senior disciple, has been a major support throughout the preparation and publication process. Her loving oversight and her diligence as director of The Cross and The Lotus Publishing supports us each step of the way.

Rebecca Harvey has been an ongoing major link to data collection and historical document searches. She seems to know just where to find more information on most everything we need. Her keen eye also provides an astute read that catches the forever-escaping grammatical challenges. Mira Lutz, our other Team-David member for the Discourses, has an excellent knowledge of grammar. It is a gift of Grace to have such a fine team working to prepare and publish Yogacharya David's series of six Discourse volumes.

Our team also includes my editor, Zia Cole, for all of the Discourse volumes—our gratitude to her for her astute eye and professional expertise.

Jan Westendorp of Kato Design and Photo brings her artistic and professional book-design expertise forward working on our manuscripts. She provides elegant page layout and image refinement support, and in so many other ways, is helping us create a beautiful series of six volumes.

Team-David feels that Yogacharya David would be delighted to know that his unique writings and teachings are available in book form for all who seek a deeper, sacred understanding of the human condition.

About the Author

Yogacharya David Hickenbottom (1954–2019) met his guru Yogacharya Mother Hamilton, a disciple of Paramhansa Yogananda, when he was a youth of 20. Yogacharya David became a Reverend in 1984 and Mother Hamilton bestowed the Yogacharya title to him in 1989.

The great Kriya Yoga lineage of India that came through Jesus, Babaji, Lahiri Mahasaya, and Sri Yukteswar to Yogananda and then to Mother Hamilton provides pathways to an appreciation of, and a faith in, the everyday sacred, to an understanding of higher dimensional wisdom, to an integral intuitive knowing of spiritual truths, and to the vibratory realms that permeate all that is, was, and will be.

Yogacharya David says: "An inner pain brought me to the path most unwillingly, and this inner pain kept me on the path. I put my shoulder to the wheel." Yogacharya David faced the crux of the spiritual dilemma—how to shift from the ego-driven lower or smaller human nature to a larger and luminous existence intuitively attuned to one's deeper and broader—vast—spiritual nature, thereby discovering the living nature of Truth. This intense striving for Truth and Bliss, and his guru's Grace, carried him through many years of spiritual experiences in the Mystical Crucifixion. His year in silence (2000–2001) established an inner state of stillness that never left him—finally attaining his full Realization.

ALSO BY YOGACHARYA DAVID

2013–2019 Discourses Series:

- *Discourses—Volume One: 2013–14: Living a Spiritually Rich Life*

- *Discourses—Volume Two: 2015: Re-Union of Soul and Spirit*

- *Discourses—Volume Three: 2016: A True New Birth*

- *Discourses—Volume Four: 2017: Gateway to the Infinite*

- *Discourses—Volume Five: 2018: Standing on the Threshold of Eternity*

- *Discourses—Volume Six: 2019: Writing in the Book of Life*

Hickenbottom, Yogacharya David. (2022). *Touching the Supreme Spirit.* Infinite Calendar. Camano Island, WA.: The Cross and The Lotus Publsihing.

Hickenbottom, Yogacharya David. (2022). *Silence: Entering the Cosmic Sea of Consciousness.* Camano Island, WA.: The Cross and The Lotus Publishing.

Hickenbottom, Yogacharya David. (2022). *Notes to Sadhakas.* Camano Island, WA.: The Cross and The Lotus Publishing.

Hickenbottom, Yogacharya David. (2021). *Climbing the Sacred Mountain: Poems and Prayers of a Western Yogi.* Camano Island, WA.: The Cross and The Lotus Publishing.

Hickenbottom, Yogacharya David. (2019). *My Spiritual India.* Camano Island, WA.: The Cross and The Lotus Publishing.

www.ingramcontent.com/pod-product-compliance
Lightning Source LLC
Chambersburg PA
CBHW070906120626
46546CB00001B/155